# FALCONRY REFLECTIONS

Dedicated to my parents
and to all falconers who enjoy
the falcon's flight

# FALCONRY REFLECTIONS

*Bob Dalton*

FARMING PRESS

First published 1997

ISBN 0 85236 372 9


A catalogue record for this book is available
from the British Library




**Published by Farming Press**
**Miller Freeman Professional Ltd**
**Wharfedale Road, Ipswich IP1 4LG, United Kingdom**


Distributed in North America
by Diamond Farm Enterprises,
Box 537, Alexandria Bay, NY 13607, USA


Cover photographs by Bob Dalton
Chapter heading illustrations:
1, 4 and 7, Ron David Digby
2, 3 and 9, Andrew Ellis
5, 6 and 8, Jim Naylor
Cover design by Mark Beesley
Typeset by Galleon Typesetting, Ipswich
Printed and bound in Great Britain by
Biddles Ltd, Guildford and King's Lynn

# CONTENTS

CHAPTER ONE

# Remus, the red headed merlin

REMUS was the little falcon with whom my career in falconry really began. But the gap between first handling a hawk and being filled with the desire to own one, to the arrival of this little falcon, was about six-and-a-half years. I had always had an extra special interest in predators in general and raptors in particular. I have a very early childhood memory of being in the garden with my father while he dug a large hole. Sparrows were feeding around the hole and from nowhere a blue streak shot into view and grabbed one of them. I was thrilled and spent the rest of the day looking at bird books until I found a picture of a musket. Whether it was this that sparked my initial interest or not I don't know, but the more I read about hawks the more I wanted to know. Then, when I discovered that there were people who trained and flew them, I knew I had to experience this first hand.

Like most would-be participants in the sport, I spent years plaguing any falconers I came across. I would travel any distance and carry out any task, no matter how menial, for the opportunity of seeing a hawk fly – even if it was only for exercise.

Some falconers were extremely kind and tolerated me tagging along and asking endless, probably inane, questions. Others definitely took advantage and got me to do their cleaning of weatherings etc. with very little, if any, reward at the end of it. I didn't mind helping with daily chores in return for gaining experience and was happy just

I

to be around hawks and falconers. But when you are young and desperate to learn you are decidedly gullible and ripe for those who wish to benefit from your inexperience. Fortunately the few who did take advantage were far outweighed by those happy to pass on their knowledge and see their sport live in another generation. You just have to shrug your shoulders and put these things down to experience.

I was, however, fortunate enough to have the opportunity of going out with falconers who flew peregrines, goshawks, sparrow-hawks, merlins gyr falcons and various foreign raptors. Quarry flown ranged from rabbit and moorhen to partridge and rook, with just about all that could be flown in between. One of the very few flights that I didn't get to see in those early days was the flight at grouse. I didn't know enough at the time to realise I had been fortunate enough to witness some first class falconry. One lesson that I certainly wasn't experienced enough at the time to under-stand was that you can tell a good falconer more by the slips he refuses than by those he decides to take on. I can recall spending an entire afternoon walking round with a falconer who was flying a female peregrine. I pointed out group after group of rooks and was told that they were too close to cover, or the wind was wrong. I honestly thought that he was afraid to let his falcon go. My feelings must have shown because he took the time and trouble to explain to me why he had not flown. He had not wanted to discourage his falcon by giving her slips with little or no chance of success. He was right and I was totally wrong. The following day we were out again and the peregrine killed a rook in fine style. This particular falconer taught me a great deal about hawks, but he also taught me about quarry. He used to quiz me about rooks and their natural history, explaining that if I hoped to hunt something successfully I should study its habits and lifestyle.

One of the falconers who was kind enough to tolerate me and take me under his wing flew red headed merlins, diminutive little falcons from Africa and India. The main quarry flown was starlings and I spent many happy weekends pursuing them with vigour. As time went on I was allowed to carry one of the red heads and eventually fly him. This, apparently, was my reward for diligently doing what I was told without grumbling and for never missing an opportunity to go out with the falcons. Mistakes I made were gently – and not so gently on some occasions – pointed out to me and my own skills in handling falcons were gradually improved.

My personal circumstances dictated that it wasn't possible for me to have a falcon of my own. I would not have been in a position to exercise it on a daily basis, or look after it properly. This situation continued from school life into working years until I had had enough of not having my own falcon to hunt. I had carried on hunting with my mentor at weekends and whenever I could sneak off school at first, then work in later days.

I decided that I needed to alter my circumstances so that I could devote time to falconry every day. I therefore changed jobs, taking a lesser paid one that would give me a great deal more time. Most importantly, it would give me daylight hours in the winter. To say that my parents were not best pleased would be an understatement. I built a secure weathering and made some decent night quarters. My mind was made up that it would be a falcon that resided in them, not a hawk. For some reason, which is impossible to put into words, hawks just did not hold the appeal for me that falcons did, nor did I get as much pleasure from the hunting flights of the hawk family. So it was to be a falcon – but which one?

The area I lived in at the time was open enough to fly smaller falcons, and starlings abounded. With the experience I had gained from my tutor, a red headed merlin seemed the obvious choice. Writing now, it seems amazing that a red head was a far easier option than a European merlin. At the time there were no such things as domestically produced hawks and all falconers' hawks came from the wild, either under licence as an eyass from this country, or as passage hawks from abroad. Unfortunately the people who sold passage hawks also sold haggards. I have never been happy with the thought of haggards being taken from the wild. After all, they were the breeding stock and I felt they should be left alone. So if it had to be a foreign hawk, it was definitely to be a passager.

I very gradually got all the necessary equipment together. Thirty years ago this was a lot more difficult than it is today. Nowadays the would-be falconer merely has to send for the various equipment suppliers' catalogues. Having chosen the one he wishes to deal with he has merely to pick up the telephone. His flexible friend will take a bit of a battering but everything will very shortly be delivered to his door. There were nowhere near the number of suppliers then in the field that there are now, and the majority who were in existence were abroad. Most equipment then had to be self-made or tracked down. Suitable scales, swivels and baths were particularly difficult to obtain, but eventually all was gathered together and I started to look around for a suitable falcon.

Being inexperienced I was highly unlikely to be granted a licence by the Home Office to take an eyass merlin, so that left the falconry column of the pets section in *Exchange and Mart*, the only publication of the period to carry advertisements for hawks and falconry equipment. At the time a red head was around £4 to £5. This may seem ridiculously little, but at the time I was earning £5 a week. One of the people advertising red heads was known to me: I had been out with him a few times to watch his hawks fly. A phone call to my tutor reassured him that I would look after the falcon properly and this led to me collecting the hawk the following Saturday.

The asking price was £4, and on collection of my falcon the seller gave me, by way of discount, a hood which I was assured fitted the falcon perfectly. Although gladly accepted at the time, I have to be honest and say I never did manage to get it onto his head. I never realised how much a small falcon could bob, weave and duck when it wanted to. But more of that later. For some reason the name Remus suggested itself and so it became.

Remus was in relatively poor feather condition, having been caught by bird trappers in India using bird lime. This really is a vile substance that ruins a hawk's plumage until it has been moulted out. It is similar to a crude contact adhesive and is liberally spread over some bent twigs that have been placed around a suitable decoy bird, such as a sparrow or a starling. When the falcon comes in to strike its tail and wing tips make contact with the twigs and then the bird is held fast. The more it struggles the more it becomes glued to the twigs. If the falcon were to be washed in a suitable agent immediately then most of the bird lime would come off and the resulting feather damage would be negligible. But of course the trappers just boxed the hawks up as they were and sent them to their respective buyers.

By the time the hawks had been gathered in India, shipped to England and distributed to the various buyers, the damage was irreversible. The only options were imping the breakages or waiting for a full moult to be completed. In the case of Remus I managed to cadge some European merlin feathers and with help he was duly imped up. At least he had a full set of flight feathers, even if the colour combinations were somewhat strange.

It seems strange that this current generation of falconers have grown into their sport not knowing what flying a red head is like. In the 1960s and early 70s red heads and luggers were extremely common, both here and on the continent. This abundance was probably one of the reasons why falconers at the time did not try to concentrate any breeding efforts on them. When import licensing was introduced in the early 1970s people rushed to get pairs of peregrines and goshawks together. Those hawks that were considered common and in use every day were more or less ignored. This has led to a situation where a red headed merlin currently costs four to five times what a peregrine does. In fact tiercel peregrines are cheaper than lugger and lanner falcons, a truly ridiculous state of affairs.

As my experience in the falconry field grew I, like many others, sought out addresses in India and Africa and ordered my own falcons direct from the trappers and dealers. Back in those supposed good old days you could literally pick up the phone and, after a long and extremely disjointed conversation with someone in India, order ten more falcons. You never actually got what you ordered, you got what the trappers managed to acquire at the time. Friends and I would work out what falcons and hawks we required and place an order accordingly, then we would sit back and wait to see what was actually sent. I can well remember an occasion when I had ordered six red heads and received four and two red naped shaheens. Not only did I get two shaheens for eight pounds, I also received a letter of apology from the supplier for not filling my order as requested. He hoped that the substitutes would prove acceptable. Needless to say I thought that they did.

Red heads were abundant in the wild, in those days, and apart from specifically requesting that no haggard birds be sent, no qualms were felt about having wild taken stock. Now things have changed and red heads, and indeed luggers, are nowhere near as common as they were then. When I talk to younger falconers today about flying red heads they look at me strangely. Unless the situation with regard to breeding them domestically changes considerably, they will never experience the pleasure of their own Remus.

Training duly started and I reduced Remus by a quarter ounce to six-and-a-half ounces. He started to feed on the fist and would even jump to it from the block, but it has to be said that in all honesty I made a pig's ear of training my first falcon. The major mistake I made was losing confidence the first time I tried to hood Remus. Because he resisted by doing an impersonation of a snake and I could not manage to get the hood anywhere near the front of his face, let alone on his head, I decided to leave this exercise until we had more confidence in each other. It was a very bad mistake and one that a lot of beginners tend to make. Leaving making a falcon to the hood till it is more settled means that it can concentrate all its efforts on dodging it. It is far better to persevere while the falcon is still in awe of you and a little scared. But these are the sorts of lessons that only experience teaches. It is so easy to be wise with the benefit of hindsight.

That is one of the things that struck me about falconry books. They never ever point out what can go wrong and the sort of mistakes the authors made in their time. After all, we are all human and we all make mistakes. How much better it would be if some of these were imparted to the tyro. First, they might well avoid a pitfall or two if authors were totally honest, and also they would not feel that they must be awful because they make mistakes and, it would appear from the writings, that others don't.

So now I had a lovely little falcon that was starting to come to the lure on the creance but I could not, no matter how patiently I tried, hood. But I had, to some degree, compensated for this by manning him very thoroughly indeed, so transporting him backwards and forwards to the flying ground did not present a problem. My second mistake was delaying flying him loose. It was obvious that he was ready to go free, but I kept finding excuses to delay the great day. I would set out saying to myself that if he came immediately the first time I would fly him loose the second, but having called Remus off once I would find a reason to put the first free flight off yet again. I was very imaginative in my excuses. It would be too windy, too still, too warm, too cold – too anything would do.

This pathetic situation could, and probably would, have gone on forever had not a friend called over on the off-chance of seeing Remus fly. The four of us set out: Remus, myself, my friend and of course the trusty creance. I called Remus off and he came a hundred yards instantly. My friend casually commented that it did not seem much of a challenge, flying the falcon on a long bit of string. I felt so ashamed and so embarrassed that I made up my mind to fly him loose there and then. No more putting off the day, no more excuses. My heart was in my mouth as I removed his leash and swivel and put him down on a fence post completely free. As I walked away from him and got the lure out of my pocket I felt convinced he wouldn't be there when I turned round. But I was worrying for nothing. Needless to say, Remus was totally unaware of the mental turmoil I was going through and just flew in to the lure to get his food as normal. It was no big deal to him. Of course now that the moment had finally been faced it came as a massive anti-climax. The only noticeable difference was that Remus came in a lot faster and slightly higher. But then he was bound to, because he did not have a great length of creance dragging him down.

The bad side of taking so long to get him completely free was that Remus did not want to work for the lure. After all, he had been used to flying straight in to it once a day and then getting fed his entire meal. It took a great deal of time to get him fit and muscled up, but eventually this was achieved and we were ready to make a start hunting. I had always flown Remus to a lure with starlings' wings adorning it and during his final preparations for entering I used a dead starling as his lure.

The day prior to the first serious attempt at entering a very slight weight reduction was brought about so as to make Remus slightly keener than normal. The plan was to fly Remus at a farm where I had permission for him to hunt. The farm consisted of large fields surrounded by old-fashioned hedgerows, and starlings used the fields as feeding grounds. I thought that I would walk along the hedgerows, looking for small groups of starlings in the correct position with regard to wind direction and available cover, to slip Remus at.

When a suitable group, in the right sort of setting, was eventually spotted I slowly raised my fist above the level of the hedgerow so as to allow Remus to spot the intended victims. Before I had managed to raise my fist fully to the height I intended, Remus bobbed his head, and with a flick of his wings was gone. I ran back a few yards to where I had noticed a gap in the hedge that I could get through easily. As I crashed through the gap I noticed that the starlings lifted off and went. Something was not right. It should not have been me that made them take flight. It should have been my falcon homing in on them with deadly intent that made them go. But Remus was not to be seen anywhere. I whistled and called but there was no response. It was no good listening for a bell as I had not put one on Remus due to his diminutive size. Telemetry in those days was unheard of.

Then I saw him, sitting on the ground not ten feet from the hedge. He was sitting as proud as punch on his first kill, happily pluming it: a sparrow. Hardly a taxing flight, or a very exciting one. In fact, other than leaving the fist I had not seen any of it. But at least he had killed and we were on our way. He was easy to make in to and allowed me to help him feed. I let him take his pleasure on the sparrow and then took him up on the fist to finish his meal. He made no attempt to shield the kill from me, or carry it, so I was content with that part of his training. I still felt proud and very pleased that Remus had had a success, albeit a very minor one. His next flight, however, was a good one at a starling. Although he was unsuccessful he chased very hard and persevered and it was only the starling's experience which saved it. The next three flights also ended in failure, but Remus was learning all the time and his luck had to change soon. It was important to achieve a success in the early days so that Remus would not become discouraged and give up trying to fly starlings.

His next flight was a cracker. We were back at the farm again and employing the hedgerow tactics that had resulted in the sparrow. After rejecting several possible slips as the flocks were too large I finally settled on a small group of about fifteen or so. I decided early on that large flocks of starlings would probably be too confusing for Remus and were therefore to be avoided. The ideal would be a family group of four or five, but these were rarely to be found in ideal circumstances. I slowly raised my fist so as to allow Remus to see his intended quarry.

Remus bobbed his head a couple of times in that strange way that falcons do. A quick look over his shoulder, another bob of the head and he was off in pursuit. The starlings took to the wing and flew directly into the wind, rising gradually as they went. They were obviously making for a stand of trees that were a good way off. Remus got in among them before they made the safety of their intended sanctuary. This gave them no option but to turn down-wind and make a straight run for it. Remus turned and gave chase. He had singled out his intended victim and was closing on it, but the starling used every ounce of its knowledge of flight and temporarily managed to avoid the attentions of his pursuer.

The starling managed to get some distance between himself and Remus, then turned again and head for its original refuge in the trees. Remus turned and chased for all he was worth. When the starling was less than fifty yards from the trees he turned it down-wind again. Now the chase was really on in earnest and eventually Remus managed to grab the starling and bring it to the ground. It was a really good flight that had ended in success for the little falcon. His chest was heaving with all the exertion as he sat astride his well-deserved kill. Mine was heaving with pride. Perhaps I was now on the right path to becoming a falconer.

My little falcon very soon became extremely adept at flying starlings and his success rate was about one in seven. He always grabbed them in flight, never putting in any sort of stoop at them. Occasionally he would spot sparrows or other small birds near the hedgerow, as I raised my fist up gently to slip him. These were never good flights, but there wasn't any real way of discouraging them other than picking him up off them without rewarding him.

9

This was not something I wanted to do because it might break the bond that was forming between us. It did mean, though, that if we had one of these incidental flights, and a kill was the result, then that was the flying over for the day. By the time the falcon had taken his reward from the kill and then his pick-up piece, the edge had most definitely gone from his appetite.

But this was not a problem that we encountered too often. As his confidence grew at starlings he would take on increasingly longer slips at them and would tend to ignore smaller birds in favour of them. His flying powers got better and better and we were now enjoying real sport as opposed to smash and grab type flights. In flight he was like a long winged sparrowhawk, faithfully following every twist and turn. He always flew directly at his quarry and tried to grab it, never attempting to make any height and never putting in a stoop. But having perused every available piece of reading matter regarding the species, it would appear this is how they hunted in the wild.

Unfortunately our first season together was brought to a premature close when Remus suffered a bout of coccidiosis. What brought this about I do not know. With hindsight it may well have been that I fed him up on his kills and he may have picked something up from one of them. Veterinary medicine for raptors was a lot less advanced then than it is now and consequently Remus took a long time to recover fully. As it was by now almost April I decided to put him down to moult, more to give him a chance to build up body strength than merely to replace feathers, although his combination plumage, while still colourful, was starting to look decidedly scruffy.

The following August I took Remus up again and commenced his retraining. Eight days later he was flying free again. No over-zealous application of the creance this time around: another seven days saw him muscled up and ready to start flying quarry again. The little falcon caught his first starling of the new season at the third time of asking. He flew with a lot more panache and his score started to mount steadily. The difference in his strength and per-severance made me wonder just how long he had been unwell the previous season before the symptoms manifested themselves.

Perhaps if my eye had been more experienced I might have picked up on it sooner, I honestly don't know.

Our second season together was proving to be a successful one and the flights had a quality to them that we had previously lacked. The highlight of his career, at least as far as I was concerned, happened a couple of months after we had recommenced hunting together. He flew a small group of starlings and failed to take one before they put in to some farm buildings. Remus landed on the apex of a barn. He was looking all around and bobbing his head. Seconds later he was off again. I naturally assumed he was in pursuit of another group of starlings. I ran round the barn and found him close to the base of it, being dragged along by a collared dove he had grabbed. It was obviously far too large for him to deal with, but he was determined not to let go of his prize. I ran up and assisted him with it. I am not sure who was more surprised that he had managed to hold it until my arrival. He subsequently tried twice more to catch one before giving them up as a bad job. Things were, in general though, going from strength to strength.

Just after Christmas, however, disaster overtook us, for Remus took ill again and died very quickly. I had flown him on Boxing Day and he had caught his quarry without too much difficulty, although he did seem very out of breath for a flight that hadn't been particularly arduous. He also took a long time to break into the quarry and did not eat with his normal gusto. I took him home and fed him up on mice, as these were a higher quality food for him. They were also a food that he normally relished and I was very disturbed when he did not even attempt to take a full crop. The next morning I collected a mute sample from him and set off to the local vet to get it analysed. I did not put him out to weather as I thought he would be better off in the warm and out of any wind. The journey to the surgery and back took less than forty minutes, but on my arrival home Remus had passed away.

I was exceedingly upset and even now, after all these years, can remember exactly how I felt when I first saw him laying there beside his indoor block. I was utterly devastated. Although it was only our second season together we had shared so much. Remus had certainly taught me far more than I ever taught him. Thoughts of replacing him just didn't enter my head for a long time. In fact I burnt all his equipment so that there wouldn't be a daily reminder of him. The only thing I kept was the hood that I never managed to fit on to him and some photographs. The hood still holds pride of place in my collection, but the photographs are getting faded and dog-eared. Until my last house move I still had my hawking diaries from those far-off days and often used to reread them and relive some of the flights we enjoyed together. But the memory of him will be with me always. I did eventually replace Remus in the mews, but not in my feelings.

At the time of writing I am flying a female red head that has been very kindly loaned to me by the Welsh Hawking Centre. She is of the African variety, which is slightly different to the Indian species, and she was actually bred here in the UK. Fortunately she didn't have to suffer the indignities and indecisiveness of my lack of experience when trained, although it is fair to say she is very bad to the hood. She arrived in feather perfect condition, not having undergone the bird lime treatment. Ruby, as she is called, flies well and catches starlings on a regular basis. She flies around the eight-and-a-half ounce mark, so has that little bit more weight than Remus. She never needs my help when it comes to despatching her quarry as did Remus, due to his slightly smaller size, although I always felt that this act helped to build the bond between us. He would struggle with a starling and even lost a few on the ground, so he knew my approach meant that he was going to receive help and that he was not going to be robbed of his prize. Also, I always fed him up on a kill so he knew that hanging on and letting me assist him was going to lead to a large, warm meal. I often wondered what I must have looked like to any passers-by: a six-foot man, lying on the ground, helping a six-ounce bird to feed.

Ruby doesn't need my help and she always has to be approached with great care. Not that she is capable of flying off with a starling, but I don't ever want her to be alarmed by my presence or sow the seeds of the vice of carrying, so I always approach her softly softly. She is very prone to sulking for some reason. Should she miss her quarry she often goes and takes stand in a tree or on a building for about half an hour or so. No amount of calling or lure swinging will induce her to return. If I leave her alone for a while and then try calling her she comes in as if nothing has happened. Her flying gives me a great deal of pleasure and flight for flight she is probably more successful than Remus ever was. But lovely though Ruby is, no falcon could ever replace Remus in my affections.

CHAPTER TWO

# Dawn, the hacked peregrine falcon

DAWN is a domestically produced peregrine falcon hatched in the second half of the 1980s. She was put out to hack with four other eyass peregrines for what should have been a two- to three-week period, but for some reason she refused to come in to the hack board after the thirteenth day. Whether she had started to kill for herself or been in some way frightened we shall never know. The outcome was that she was still in the vicinity and would roost with the other hack hawks, but would not come in and feed from the hack board. Obviously if you put a falcon out to hack then you run the risk that they may kill for themselves and therefore start missing the odd day at the board. But Dawn was missing every day. She was obviously more advanced than had originally been thought, because she simply refused to come in at all. The fact that she was still in the area gave hope that the first day she didn't kill for herself she would come in to the board again and thereby be taken up. And that is exactly what happened on day thirty-two.

So, some two weeks late, I found myself in possession of a peregrine falcon that had enjoyed the benefits of a really good hack. At least I could be sure she was sound of lung and well and truly muscled up. What faults she had learnt while out, if any, would presumably manifest themselves further down the road. I must admit to being worried that she might all too easily fly at check, although this should not prove to be too much of a problem on a grouse moor.

Training followed a very routine and predictable path and nothing untoward happened during this time. Dawn was initially a little wary of the pointers but extra care in this department soon saw her totally relaxed in their company. After twenty-two days she was flying loose and she joined the cadge with two other falcons as we all headed north for the annual grouse hawking pilgrimage. Although in those days I didn't go for anywhere near as long as I do now, there was still plenty of time to enter her and get her wedded to her intended quarry.

Her first season at grouse was not startling. She acquitted herself well enough, but there were no fireworks. She wasn't going to be a grouse hawk that would be forever remembered with universal admiration. But she learnt her job. She knew about finding lift and what it meant to her when a dog was on point. Her pitch was a moderate one and she had to be served relatively quickly or she would lose interest and go wandering off. This, I think, was directly related to her unintentional extended hack. As well as learning a great deal about the specifics of flying she had also learnt that she could catch things on her own without the help of man and his dog. Should it prove that man and dog were slow in assisting her then she could go off and do it all by herself. Dawn had also learnt to go and sit on a rock or a branch and take a rest if she felt so inclined. This is something that can be infuriating beyond words when you are trying to get her over a good point.

She killed a great many of her grouse because she was so big and powerful and could often fly them down, even if flushed when she was slightly out of position. Dawn flies at over two pounds six ounces and is very tenacious once the flight is on. She has achieved a lot of kills that other falcons just wouldn't make because of this characteristic. Several times grouse have flushed when she has been cruising around downwind, out of position. But the instant she has spotted them she has turned up the wick and gone into pursuit mode. She has followed them and taken one as they have attempted to put in to the safety of the heather. Not a very stylish flight, but one that she has taught herself, and it would be practically impossible to unteach her.

I remember very clearly a kill she had on a moor near

Grantown on Spey that clearly illustrates this ability of hers. I was trying to get her to come over a point that was not ideal, but better than nothing. The point was about half a mile from the edge of the moor, which then changed abruptly from open heather moorland to a dense fir plantation. As I moved to head the point another covey of grouse broke between the point the dogs were holding and the wood. The grouse duly whirred off towards the safety of the thickly grouped stand of timber. Dawn spotted them and immediately set off in pursuit. I can recall thinking that it was wasted energy on her part, but at least the trees would probably give her some decent lift for her return. Hopefully when she returned from this futile exercise she would in all probability be nicely placed for the point we had originally set out to fly.

The grouse flew into the trees just a few feet off the ground and were lost to my sight immediately. A few seconds behind them Dawn crossed the edge of the wood about eighty feet above it. That is that, I thought, and started to make my way again to the head of the point, confident that Dawn would be back overhead shortly. When I was on the right line to make my approach towards the dogs I looked around for Dawn. She was nowhere to be seen. I unslung the telemetry from my back and switched the set on. A nice steady bleep was emitting from it. Dawn was stationary. I cursed heatedly. She had probably taken stand in a tree somewhere, having failed to spot the grouse as she flew over the wood. I whistled and called, but to no avail.

I had no alternative but to go and find her. I left the dogs firmly marking the covey they had found; there was nothing to be gained by sending them in. After all, if I recovered Dawn quickly there was still the chance of getting a flight. I crossed to the wood and entered it. It was one of those modern plantations where the trees are so close together that it is difficult to walk between them. The signal was a strong one and it was obvious that Dawn wasn't very far in front of me, probably only two or three hundred yards. When I got what seemed a considerable distance into the wood it occurred to me I was going to have a devil of a job to get her down. If she was sitting near the top of one of those trees there was no way she was going to see me on the ground, much less have a clear path physically to come down to the lure.

But as the signal gained in strength it was clear that she was already on the ground. I disconnected the aerial from the telemetry set and was still getting a good clear signal. This meant she was very close indeed, probably less than twenty feet away. I got down on my hands and knees and, as I did so, I literally looked Dawn in the eye. She had indeed caught her grouse and was in one of the irrigation channels that ran through the wood. The plumage of the grouse and the bed of pine needles had muffled her bells. As she sat eating her quarry I put on her jesses, leash and swivel. When she had finished eating a good warm crop I took her up, hooded her and made my way out of the wood.

How on earth she had spotted the grouse through the dense foliage and managed to get down on it I have no idea. As we emerged from the wood we were greeted by the sight of the two pointers still holding steady. I was hot, tired and sweaty. Just about the last thing I wanted to do was to go over and head their point; I wanted to sit down in the heather and take a breather. But they had stuck to their task faithfully and so deserved a reward. I walked across and went through the motions of flushing exactly as if it were a real flight. Once the dogs had sprung the grouse they received their verbal praise, which is all they ever ask.

Over the years Dawn has gradually turned into a real journeyman falcon. She has never been truly spectacular but she can almost always be relied upon to get the job done. Many times she has been lent out to falconers who have come up to stay with me in Scotland. She is exceptionally good natured in that she will allow herself to be handled by just about anyone, but they all have to be warned what the circumstances can turn into if she misses her quarry and has to be recalled to the lure.

Dawn can, on occasions, be extremely bad-tempered to say the least. One Portuguese falconer will certainly never forget her and her tantrums. Coming directly from Portugal to Britain he obviously wasn't in a position to bring his falcon with him, due to our quarantine laws. When I offered him the opportunity to fly Dawn, rather than merely spectate, he jumped at the chance. Care had been taken to warn him of Dawn's aggressive nature should she fail with her quarry, but he either didn't listen too carefully or, more probably, thought that I was overstating the risks involved. After all, Dawn is a peregrine falcon not a golden eagle.

The Portuguese falconer put Dawn up over a point and as she worked to reach her pitch he made his way round to head the dogs. But due to a combination of excitement and inexperience he tried to head the dogs without giving the grouse in front of them sufficient leeway. Consequently the grouse jumped when Dawn was still way out of position. Despite the fact that she didn't stand a chance, Dawn still gave chase for all that she was worth. After a thoroughly futile expenditure of energy she eventually gave up, turned round and started making her way back. Knowing what this sort of situation could lead to I shouted a warning to my friend to be careful on Dawn's return. He chuckled at me, shaking his head, and proceeded to get his lure from his falconry bag.

I could tell from the speed she was coming in that Dawn had no intention of merely settling gently on her lure. Her blood was up and she was looking for something or someone to take it out on. My friend from Portugal was definitely shaping up to be it. He was happily swinging the lure and, as Dawn got closer, he threw it out onto the ground, to one side of him. At the very last minute the penny dropped, and he realised *he* was the target, not the lure. Ducking rapidly was not sufficiently evasive tactics to avoid all contact. Dawn still managed to grab the cap from his head and fly off with it clutched firmly in her feet. Once she was a good way off, and up a good height, she released the cap from her grip and only then made her way back to the lure. But the fun was not yet over. Having landed on the lure, the falconer bent down to take her up on the fist once she had finished. Dawn left the lure, lacerated his ungloved hand, and then returned to the lure to contentedly finish her meal.

The strange thing is that once she has got the aggression out of her system she is as gentle as a lamb. But, oddly enough, my friend didn't want to fly Dawn again for the rest of his stay with us. Nor did he ever find his cap.

On another occasion, when flying Dawn myself, I had reason to remember her aggression. It was late September, when grouse are notoriously twitchy and prone to jumping from the point. The dogs had managed to get a good point on the side of a gorge that had a stream running through the bottom of it. I unhooded Dawn and let her take off in her own time. Having lightened her load via the rear end and roused thoroughly she launched herself from the glove and started to work her way up over the dogs. For once she was intent on hunting, as opposed to mooching around the moor.

I, in the meantime, worked my way round to head the point. When Dawn was out of position, still working downwind to get height, the grouse jumped and made good their escape by flying down the gorge. Both pointers ran forwards a short way and then came on rigid point again. Obviously not all the grouse had taken flight. I was relieved as it meant that Dawn would get a good flight after all. But I, of all people, should have known better and been prepared for what happened next. I was so pleased to see the dogs come back on point that I made the mistake of taking my eyes off her. I merely waved my glove above my head, the normal method of getting her to fly over the top of my position.

The next thing I knew was that I received a very hard blow to the side of my head. It had sufficient strength to knock me over into the gorge. Because it came as such a surprise I was not in a position to put my hands out and save myself, and ended up lying in the bottom of the stream. As I clambered out and back up the side of the gorge I was greeted by howls of laughter from my friends. I had to wait several minutes for the mirth to abate before finding out exactly what had happened. Apparently when I started waving the glove to attract Dawn's attention that is precisely what I did. She immediately closed her wings and stooped. She hit my head with a whack that was audible to my friends some thirty feet away. On checking the side of my head I found a large lump that was bleeding very steadily. Not only had she hit me, she had managed to rake me with her talons as she went by.

It then occurred to me that I didn't know where Dawn was. According to my friends, having hit me Dawn had thrown up to a good height. I, not surprisingly, had called out as I was hit and took my tumble. This shout had motivated the dogs to flush the grouse they were pointing and Dawn had taken one out of the air very neatly as they rose. I enquired as to Dawn's whereabouts and was told she was some thirty yards away, in the heather, eating her grouse. When I asked why no one had picked her up for me I was greeted with a string of suggestions as to where I could go and what I could do when I got there.

Having made into her Dawn was back to her normal, calm, gentle self. She left her grouse and stepped gently up onto the glove for her titbit as if butter wouldn't melt in her mouth. She was completely calm and collected and it was impossible to believe this was the same falcon who had put me on my back in a stream a few minutes earlier. That is the strange thing about her. Other than when she has these odd lapses of temper she really is very mild mannered as a rule. When being taken out from the mews to her weathering, weighed and loaded up for the day's hawking she is the epitome of good manners. She only normally plays up when a flight goes wrong and she thinks the falconer is to blame.

A very close and trusted friend of mine, Roger Ratcliffe, comes up for a week or two's grouse hawking with me each season. Year after year Roger valiantly flies Dawn. Not only that, he actually *asks* if he can fly her. He puts these little temper tantrums down to high spirits and seems to enjoy them, or the result of them, when they happen. On more than one occasion he has had his hands lacerated and she has attempted to strike him several times while flying past. But still Roger loves her and loves flying her.

Another of Dawn's predilections is for taking ground game. She has killed rabbits, brown hares and blue hares. Her last blue hare was typical of her method when dealing with such quarry. We were flying up at Grantown on Spey again, on a particularly beautiful moor that overlooks the town. Dawn had put on the wing over a split point. That is, the two pointers were about twelve yards apart, but facing in different directions. My first thought was that the dogs had got themselves in among a covey of grouse that were spread out, or that they had stumbled on a pair and were pointing one each. But that was not the case.

As Dawn came overhead, in perfect position, I sent one of the pointers in to flush. Instead of a grouse a blue hare took off across the moor. Dawn put in a half-hearted stoop and then started to ring up. She went higher and higher and was still pumping up – not drifting up on thermals, but actually pumping hard in a deliberate effort to gain height. Within a few minutes she was far higher than she had ever been before. I started to worry that perhaps she was off on her way once and for all. But when I yelled and waved the glove she started to make her way back overhead. I worked my way round and faced both dogs, waiting for the ideal moment to flush. (I say both dogs, because the first that had pointed the hare had now decided to back the point that the other dog held.) So with both dogs now on the same point and myself in the right position all I had to do was wait for Dawn to place herself correctly for the flush. When things looked right I sent the dogs in.

Again a blue hare got up. I couldn't believe it. Dawn turned over and dropped like a stone. She hit the hare so hard it cartwheeled a good twenty feet over the heather. It did not move again of its own accord, but Dawn hit it again and again, at least half a dozen times. When she had successfully vented her anger on it she then came down and sat on it. Whenever she takes ground quarry she hits them repeatedly to ensure that the fight has gone out of them before she lands on them. But this time she need not have bothered. The hare was definitely dead after the initial impact.

Don't run away with the idea that Dawn is just a bruiser and is incapable of flying with great style and panache, however. Another memorable flight that sticks in my mind was when she took her first cock pheasant. I was hawking a moor in Morayshire with Trevor Hill, a falconer from Tenbury Wells. We were making our way down off the moor, having had a very unsuccessful day. Right on the edge of the moor the dogs suddenly locked on to a firm point. It was Dawn's turn to fly, so equipment was removed and off she went. She had hardly left the fist and was no more than twenty feet off the ground when a cock pheasant broke and rocketed off the moor. Dawn was facing the wrong way, but she turned and gave chase. We watched the pheasant go over a rise and out of sight. Dawn reached the same rise but instead of hugging the ground and going over, she threw up to a terrific height. She held herself momentarily and then launched into a tremendous stoop. Because of the rise in the ground Dawn was out of sight almost immediately. A few seconds later she threw up over the ridge again, held station for a couple of seconds, and then stooped again.

Trevor and I ran as fast as we could but as we cleared the rise we could not see Dawn, though we could see some sheep netting stretched out in front of us. Scattered along the fence were hawk feathers. My heart was in my mouth and, as we got closer, I could see a body at the base of the fence. It turned out to be a female sparrowhawk. Sad for the sparrowhawk, but my heart leapt for joy that it wasn't Dawn. She was a couple of hundred yards further down the slope, proudly sitting astride her cock pheasant. Needless to say Dawn was allowed to take her pleasure on it in her own time.

Throughout her career Dawn has been very adaptable, not just towards the different falconers that have handled and flown her, but also to quarry species chased. She has primarily been used as a grouse hawk, which is the reason she was obtained in the first place. But I have flown her down south at pheasant, partridge, duck and rook. Pheasants she has taken in good numbers, most in the proper style, that is waiting on over dogs. But on several occasions she has taken them directly off the fist – not something that I like to do or think is particularly sporting.

That came about because I received a telephone call from someone claiming to be the private secretary of an Arab dignitary. They asked if I could make myself available on a particular date to fly a falcon at pheasant. Apparently the Arab gentleman had some guests coming to stay and wanted to show them some hawking. I was informed that I could go down to his estate for a few days beforehand and familiarise myself and my falcons with the ground.

Two keepers greeted me on my arrival on the first of the reconnaissance forays. Despite the opinions still held by some older-school keepers, these were very keen to see a falcon fly. They were also delighted I had brought the two pointers, Emma and Evie, with me. We duly set off and had two flights at pheasant with Dawn and one more with another falcon. We managed to catch a brace of pheasant, one with each falcon, and all in all had a thoroughly good day. The following day was very similar and one pheasant was taken by Dawn. The dogs were enjoying themselves hugely as there were pheasants everywhere: the estate put down large numbers of birds and fed them well.

The private secretary met me on the eve of the big day and said that he would come out with me to discuss protocol for the following day. He also wanted to see at first hand what was going to happen and if there was anything that might upset the host and his guests.

The dogs were ruled out of the action immediately. Apparently unless a dog is a saluki it is unholy and its presence would not be tolerated. Our host was not a complete traditionalist, but one of the guests was. I get as much pleasure from seeing the dogs work as I do from seeing the falcons fly but on this estate, with its abundance of game, being without them would probably not prove a major handicap.

We set off to hawk and, instead of dogs, I used binoculars to spot feeding pheasants. Fortunately finding a pheasant in a suitable position did not prove difficult. I unhooded Dawn and cast her off. While waiting for her to gain height the secretary asked me what I was doing. I explained about the falcon gaining height and then walking into the pheasant and flushing it so that the falcon could stoop at it. Shock number two. No waiting on flights, it must be off the fist. I tried as tactfully as possible to explain that Dawn was a falcon not a goshawk and her method of flight required the advantage of height, but the secretary had seen a private video of houbara hawking in the Middle East and all the falcons on that had left the fist to attack their prey. I could not persuade him that this was a different set of circumstances and therefore required a different type of flight. He was adamant as to what was required – he found the flight fully acceptable but my host and, more importantly, his guests would not.

My big concern was that Dawn was used to waiting on flights at pheasant and probably wouldn't take them on the ground straight from the fist. I didn't feed her at all that day in the hope that the resulting sharpness the next day would induce her to try a flight that she just wasn't used to.

The following morning saw the hawking party assemble and after lengthy introductions we set off. We had only been out a few minutes when I spotted three hen pheasants feeding on a game strip near a hedge. Dawn was unhooded and I raised my fist slightly to allow her to spot the pheasant. She sat there bobbing her head but did not take off. In desperation I launched her off, something I am very loth to do, and she was soon flying towards the pheasants. I ran forward shouting and two of the pheasants just calmly scuttled into the hedge. But, fortunately for Dawn and myself, the third one took off in an attempt to clear the hedge. Dawn grabbed it and brought it to the ground, where she quickly despatched it.

Our host was extremely happy. He asked if he could fly Dawn the next time, so of course I had to say I would be honoured and handed Dawn over. We soon found another pheasant away from a hedge and Dawn was launched unceremoniously at it. This pheasant ran instead of flying and Dawn used her ground game tactics on him. She hit him several times before coming down on him. By that time the pheasant had had the stuffing knocked out of him and she very soon despatched him.

So the day ended as a success despite my previous misgivings – two flights and two pheasants in the bag. As we slowly walked back to the house for refreshments one of the guests detached himself from the party and came to talk to me. This was the 'honoured guest' who was a true traditionalist when it came to Arab ways. He told me how much he had enjoyed the flights, and expressed the opinion that Dawn was a fine, large falcon and certainly brave. But one thing puzzled him. He had been grouse hawking in Scotland many times and felt he had to ask me whether I might not get better sport using pointers and waiting on flights. When I explained the situation and how it had unfolded over the previous couple of days he laughed till the tears ran down his cheeks.

Since that day he has invited me many times to hawk with him, both here and in Scotland. I often lend him a falcon to fly, but never Dawn in case she throws one of her temper tantrums at him. We have also flown ducks with Dawn on this gentleman's estate and more than once he has waded out into the water to get the ducks to rise under Dawn. When it comes to falconry he is as keen as anybody I have ever met. He has tried many times to buy Dawn off me but has now resigned himself to the fact that he may have one of her offspring in the future.

Dawn has also flown rook on many occasions, but it is not a quarry that she relishes. She has to be reduced a couple of ounces in weight to take them on. She deals with rooks very easily once she does take them on, though, and has never ever needed my assistance in despatching them.

The only care I have to take when flying Dawn is other raptors. She has an absolute hatred of them, chasing peregrines, buzzards, harriers and kestrels with a vengeance. Needless to say I don't want her or them hurt so I have to try and ensure that none are in the area when I cast her off.

Dawn and I have had a good career together, with many interesting flights. The high spots have always far outweighed any low ones. We have both been fortunate that she has only ever had one major illness and she recovered fully from this thanks to the attention of a very skilled vet. For the last year or so I have had the feeling that she has worked hard enough and perhaps it is now time life was easier for her. This is probably misguided sentimentality on my part but it is a feeling that won't go away. Consequently Dawn is now in official retirement. She is on loan to Cerri Griffiths at the Welsh Hawking Centre in the hopes of producing some offspring. If she does it will be interesting to see if they inherit her temperament. My heart hopes that they do. My hands hope that they don't.

# CHAPTER THREE

# Shakey, the tiercel red naped shaheen

M OST falconers can look back on their hawking careers and there will be one or two particular hawks or falcons that stand out head and shoulders above the rest. Whether it is because they were brilliant performers in the field or perhaps because they were exceptionally brave, they will always be remembered with that extra little bit of warmth and affection.

In my case a falcon that will always be remembered with fondness is Shakey, a tiercel red naped shaheen. His hunting partnership with me lasted just three-and-a-half years, but they were very exciting and very rewarding years from a falconer's point of view.

I have always had a soft spot for flying the smaller species of peregrine and therefore shaheens, red or black, barbaries and brookeis have been among my favourite falcons. Some of the traditional works on falconry decry these birds because of their diminutive size and some even go so far as to question their bravery and effectiveness as hunters. How thoroughly ridiculous. If they were as slack mettled as these works would have us believe then they would have died out in the wild a very long time ago.

I had not had the opportunity to fly a red naped shaheen since the days when imported passage and haggard falcons were the norm. It would therefore be interesting for me to see how a domestically produced falcon would compare with its wild counterpart.

27

Shakey was bred here in England from parents that had been wild taken in Saudi Arabia and then brought over here on their owner's return. He was one of a clutch of three and the breeder had decided to retain one falcon and one tiercel for future breeding stock. A chance glimpse of an advert, very late in the season, for a shaheen led to the initial call. I was told it had been sold but to call back in a couple of days, just in case the prospective buyer failed to collect.

Having duly called back some three days later, just on the off-chance, I discovered the proposed buyer *had* failed to show up and that the tiercel shaheen was still for sale. A collection date and time were arranged and several days later I headed north to collect the new member of my hawking team.

When I arrived at the breeder's the young tiercel was still in the aviary with his parents. The breeder and I caught him up and put on his equipment. It was a six-hour trip home and I decided to leave the newcomer hooded on an indoor block for the night. This was so that he had a chance to settle down before training commenced the next day.

On the following morning, as soon as he was unhooded, Shakey suggested his own name. Like a great many falcons he shook when nervous, but this falcon shook so violently he almost fell off the fist. But this shaking could not have been purely from nerves as Shakey fed on the fist the first time of asking. In fact all his training progressed in copy book style and I can say with hand on heart that we never faltered, not even momentarily. In just eleven days from that first morning Shakey was coming instantly the full length of the creance. Not only that, he was good to pick up off the lure and hooded impeccably. So the next day he was flown free. Even after a great many years as a falconer, and with a lot of trained hawks to my credit, this is still very much a heart in the mouth experience. But Shakey behaved well and after a few circuits came in instantly when the lure was produced. Within a few days of free flight he seemed to be strong on the wing and flying with confidence. He was using the wind wisely and gaining height with relative ease. All the indications were that he was ready to be entered at quarry.

The partridge season was underway and they were a quarry of which there were large numbers on the ground I hunted. Friends felt that with a flying weight of just sixteen-and-a-quarter ounces Shakey might be too small to be able to deal with them effectively. I had no such doubts and was determined to fly him at them. With the help of Emma the pointer I was confident that the three of us would have some good sport as well as a great deal of fun.

The next afternoon we set out to hunt partridge with a fair degree of confidence. It was one of those days when you cannot seem to find a decent point. All too soon the light was starting to fade and I was almost on the point of putting Shakey on the wing for some exercise. Then Emma provided us with a good, usable point. Scanning the ground ahead of her with a pair of binoculars revealed a covey of English partridge. They were clustered around the bottom of a hedgerow on the edge of a freshly ploughed field. It was a case of now or never as far as this particular day was concerned. Another ten or fifteen minutes and there would be insufficient light to fly.

Shakey was put on the wing and he started to mount nicely. Not to a terrific height, but he was waiting on relatively tightly. All the time he was circling, his head was turned in towards me, watching what was going on. When he seemed to have reached his pitch, I waited till he was in the optimum position and then Emma and I rushed in from opposite sides and flushed the partridge. Shakey stooped immediately and contact was made with his quarry.

However, because the light was failing and both falcon and partridge were against the background of ploughed earth they disappeared from view. I squatted down in order to have some sky as background, but I could not see either bird break the skyline. I was not sure whether Shakey had come down with his partridge or whether he had tail chased it over the next hedgerow. Standing on the headland of the field I swung the lure and called. If Shakey had missed the partridge he would come back in to the lure. If not, then surely sooner or later his bells would give his position away.

After several minutes, which seemed more like an eternity, there was still no sign of Shakey, but twice I thought I heard the tinkle of bells. The receiver for the telemetry was back in the car but I decided against going back to get it as I felt sure that my little falcon was close by. Again I caught the tinkle of a bell on the wind. I started to make my way gradually forward, stopping and listening every few yards. The light was going all too quickly for my liking. I began sweeping the ground with my binoculars in an attempt to locate Shakey.

Out of the corner of my eye I caught sight of a few feathers drifting on the wind. I swept the glasses over the ground in the direction of the feathers and, lo and behold, there was Shakey pluming his quarry. I was over the moon with joy. Not only had I found my falcon but he had also killed a partridge at his first attempt. So much for his being too small.

I started to walk towards him and he immediately froze and crouched down on his prey. When I stopped still he stood up again and recommenced feeding. I went forward – and he crouched and froze again. No wonder I had experienced difficulty in finding him, even though he was less than thirty yards from me when I first started looking for him. This was a characteristic he was to repeat when on quarry again and again. I suppose it was some sort of throwback to natural behaviour patterns, hiding himself and his prey from a would-be predator.

But at least our partridge hawking career together was off to a good start. Shakey managed to catch the next eleven partridge in a row, without a miss. Whenever I could get a decent point on partridge then Shakey was the falcon to be flown. I must admit he did get preferential treatment over the other falcon I was flying at the time. After he had gained in both confidence and ability I was able to switch him to hedgerow hawking on days when we couldn't find good points on partridge. Starlings became our main quarry on these occasions. The success rate at these was very good and the season's combined total score was rising steadily. Not that falconry should be about achieving large scores. But if you have a falcon that flies with style, then the two things normally go hand in hand.

In the latter part of November I got the opportunity to fly Shakey on a large sporting estate in Caithness. I jumped at the chance and duly headed north with a cadge of falcons that included the little shaheen. Apparently this estate consisted of a decent stretch of moorland with good numbers of red grouse as well as some arable land that held partridge. As so often happens in

Scotland, the weather at this time of the season took a turn for the better and we enjoyed a particularly good, if somewhat short, spell. Bright sunny days with good strong winds: ideal for falconers that wait on and good scenting conditions for the pointers.

As things turned out, the chance to fly at partridge was nonexistent and so I decided to take Shakey up onto the moor for some exercise. His bravado when flying partridge led me to believe that he had earned at least one chance at grouse, even though in theory he stood absolutely no chance at all of hitting one or holding one. To cut a long story short, Shakey was given a chance at this quarry and he gave it all he was worth. He went up well over the point and fought the elements to keep himself in position in relation to the pointer. Unfortunately the grouse jumped prior to being flushed and, although not ideally placed, Shakey put in a tremendous stoop at the fleeing pair and made contact with the lead one. The grouse faltered in flight but managed to keep going and make good its escape.

I was like a dog with two tails. To see this tiny little falcon give his all in trying to catch a quarry larger than himself really filled me with pride. Unfortunately the weather reverted to its seasonal norm the next day and that put an end to our chances of trying again at grouse for that season. I made up my mind there and then that the following August would see myself and Shakey back in Scotland, to give him a fair crack at grouse over a decent period. Not just an odd day here or there, but a proper eight-week spell.

On my return down south I had an invitation to attend a field meeting of the Welsh Hawking Club at Abersoch, North Wales, so Shakey and I headed for the meet where the main quarry was to be partridge. On the first day I drew first flight. With other members of the field we made our way to an area where, apparently, partridge were known to be. Shakey was put on the wing and despite a literal gale blowing, he kept good position and mounted to a very good pitch. Regardless of the assurances of our field leader there were not actually any partridge present or any signs of them. Shakey decided to take matters into his own hands and put in a long shallow stoop at a flock of starlings that were feeding about three-quarters of a mile away.

It was obvious from his tremendous throw up back into the sky that he had failed to catch one. But instead of coming back in to the lure, he was off like a rocket at another flock that were rapidly disappearing over a distant hill. I waited for a few minutes, calling and swinging the lure, but Shakey did not reappear. So it was out with the tracking gear to see which direction he had gone in once he was out of my sight. I got a signal, but it was a very weak one and getting weaker. I ran back across the fields to the car and set off in the direction of the rapidly fading bleep. Now every book ever written about falconry will tell you that when a falcon goes off it does so downwind (because, presumably, this is the line of least resistance). I set off downwind and had soon lost the signal altogether. I decided to drive round in ever increasing circles till I picked a signal up again. After some fifty minutes I did manage to get a signal which was actually gaining in strength. On investigation I came across a party flying a golden eagle and it was fitted with an identical transmitter to Shakey. I explained the situation to them and they very kindly removed the batteries from their transmitter so that I could carry on trying to track down my wayward falcon.

Some five hours later Shakey was tracked down to an island seven miles upwind from where he had last been seen. The island was a mile offshore and the sea in between looked pretty inhospitable. Now all that had to be done was to find someone with a motor boat who was willing to take a mad falconer out to an island to get his falcon back. The boat owner obviously thought he was dealing with someone who was a few cells short in the brain department. The price was outrageous, but what choice was there? I wanted my falcon back. Once safely back on the fist again, Shakey was officially grounded until the next grouse hawking season.

It seemed to take forever for 12 August to come back round again. But eventually it did and Shakey, Emma the pointer and I were ready to go. The general consensus of opinion among my fellow falconers about me trying to catch grouse with a tiercel shaheen ranged from pity to sheer ridicule. Only one whom I spoke to thought we stood even a remote chance and he was convinced that if we did get one it would be by grabbing the grouse as they tried to put in – not in flight fair and square with a stoop. One other falconer did wish me luck, but I have the feeling that this was slightly tongue in cheek. The Glorious Twelfth fell on a Sunday that year so we waited till Monday to start our campaign. Although it is legal to hunt grouse in Scotland on a Sunday I preferred not to as the locals in the area of this particular moor did not like it. What is the point of upsetting the local community you intend to spend the next eight weeks among, purely for the sake of one day's hawking?

The first four days that we tried to catch a grouse were filled with nothing but sheer frustration. The grouse would not lay to the point, or they would jump as the falcon was being cast off the fist. Whatever the reasons, we set out on the fifth day having not had a single decent crack at grouse. The first point of this day followed the pattern of the previous days. Just as I had unhooded the falcon, the covey in front of the dog jumped and flew into the distance, uttering that irritating cackle they are so fond of giving. Is it just me or does this cackle sound as though the grouse are laughing at the falconer?

Fortunately Emma did not get frustrated and continued to work with her normal vigour and enthusiasm. She came on point again and it was obvious from the way she was holding her head that the grouse were some way in front of her. Perhaps this time they would hold and we would actually get a flight. I unhooded Shakey and hoped he would take off fairly quickly. His presence in the air above the grouse would help to persuade them to stay where they were. I say I hoped he would take off quickly as I do not believe in launching my falcons off the fist, preferring to let them have a look around and take off in their own time.

Shakey roused and took off after what seemed an age. It was probably only thirty seconds or so, but it seemed more like several minutes. All the time I was expecting the grouse to jump and ruin the party. From his days of partridge hawking, Shakey had learned that Emma was the provider of the flights and therefore he had developed the habit of ringing up into the sky directly over her. I could not ask for more, as it meant that after twenty or so seconds in the air you could more or less guarantee that he would keep the quarry pinned down. On this particular day the sun was shining and a light breeze was blowing, ideal conditions for the little falcon.

He was soon up to a nice height and waiting on nicely. As soon as he set his wings and thereby signalled that he was ready, Emma was sent in to flush. The grouse rose and immediately Shakey turned over and started to stoop. Those few seconds that it took him to come down seemed to take forever. A year's hopes and expectations were about to come to fruition. The moment of impact was one of the most exciting in my life. The grouse tumbled to earth, and it was obvious from the manner in which it fell that it had a broken wing. Shakey threw back up almost as high as his starting point. Terrified of losing the grouse I ran towards the spot where it had fallen and in doing so put up two more. They took off like bullets and again Shakey turned over and stooped. Once again he made contact and this grouse fell dead to the ground. Shakey went back up again and then, spotting his original grouse fluttering in the heather, he came down on it.

I ran over and picked up the dead one before making in to the little falcon. He sat so proudly straddling his prize. I helped him break into it and as he took his richly deserved reward of a crop of warm grouse, I refitted his jesses, leash and swivel. While he took a massive crop at his pleasure I sat in the heather filled with admiration for his determination and bravery. He had almost three-quarters of a crop before it occurred to me to take a photograph of him on his kill. That day and the feelings that flooded through me will live forever in my mind.

That night I was on the telephone to all those who had doubted the capabilities of this tiercel shaheen. I must also be honest and confess to toasting his health a great many times in the native brew and felt like death warmed up the next day. It took a long time to sink in that he had not only killed grouse at his first serious attempt, but that he had succeeded in taking a brace out of the same covey. But it did not stop there. His success continued and almost every time he got himself into a good position he killed.

This season at grouse always brings back many happy memories. Several foreign guests joined us during our eight-week campaign. The quarantine restrictions of the time meant it was not possible for any of them to bring their own falcons with them. I therefore let most of them fly Shakey so that they could experience the excitement first hand. One particular Dutch falconer who'd arrived on a

Sunday spent the day quizzing me about what to expect in terms of sport the next day. I emphasised to him that grouse hawking is a difficult branch of falconry and that he should be prepared for more disappointment than elation. When I showed him Shakey weathering on the lawn he expressed the opinion that he would not stand a chance of catching a grouse as he was far too small. I explained that he had already killed a good number and took them with style, but it was obvious from the man's expression and body language that he did not believe me.

The following day we went up onto the moor and almost immediately Emma came on point. My Dutch friend put Shakey on the wing and watched as the little falcon mounted up to a speck in the sky over the pointer. On my command Emma went in and flushed the grouse and Shakey stooped and killed the lead cock bird stone dead. The stricken grouse literally dropped at the feet of the Dutchman. Within ten minutes of being on the moor he had witnessed a spectacular flight with a successful outcome. He now said that he had not realised just how easy grouse hawking was and could not understand why everybody considered it so difficult. Needless to say after this fateful remark we did not kill another grouse for four days, but perhaps what he'd said was understandable. When falconry goes well and everything clicks into place it does look quite easy. But the nature of the sport is that it all goes wrong a lot more frequently than it goes right.

As the season continued so did Shakey's learning curve. In fact he learnt some lessons a little too well. As the season draws on grouse tend to get to a stage where they simply will not lay to a point. They invariably fly off as a pointer approaches them. The close proximity of the dog puts the grouse under pressure and they fly off to get away from it. The standard practice to get around this is to put a high mounting falcon in the air. The falcon will hold the grouse on the ground as they would rather take their chance with the dog than the falcon. I tried this a few times with Shakey but it did not work. Shakey had learnt that it was Emma who provided the grouse. If he couldn't see her on point then he would simply cruise round low or go and sit on a rock. It was seeing the dog on point that gave him the incentive to mount up high into the sky.

Another thing he taught himself was to hit the grouse on the head or the wing. With his very small size this was the only way he could effectively stop them: a blow to their body would hardly check their flight at all and he certainly did not have the bulk to bind them in mid-air and bring them down. As he had to hit them, and hit them hard, this led to some very spectacular flights.

Although he killed a good number of grouse, his habit of crouching on his kill meant that if I had not managed to mark the exact spot where he came down I had to get the telemetry out and track him. In long heather this can be a great deal more difficult than is at first imagined. It often meant that by the time I got to him he had managed to enjoy a very good crop of warm grouse which ruled him out for flying again that day. I never begrudged him his reward, but I would just rather he took it in my time than his own.

Other than the occasional field meet where partridge were to be the quarry, I kept Shakey purely for grouse. The verve and dash with which he flew this quarry impressed and gave joy to a great many people as well as myself.

During Shakey's second season at grouse I had the opportunity to go on a new moor for a couple of weeks. The only stipulation laid down by the moor owner was that his gamekeeper should accompany our party each day. It was more than obvious right from the start that the gamekeeper was not thrilled by our presence, or the prospect of our hunting his grouse. Our party consisted of me with Shakey and two other falconers, each with falcons. The keeper was singularly and obviously unimpressed by our initial efforts at sport. But as we carefully explained, it takes a while to get to know the lie of the land and, more importantly, how the wind affects the ground you are flying (that is to say, whether there are updraughts or downdraughts). By about the fourth day we were getting into our stride and Shakey had a couple of good flights and had managed to connect with a grouse, although he failed to hold it. But this flight seemed to galvanise the keeper. He started to take us to more productive areas of the moor and actually started to get excited whenever it was Shakey's turn to fly.

When we were near the end of our stay on this moor we experienced one of those days when there just isn't any scent for the dogs to work on. Although we did give them a quick run on the moor it was obvious to everyone that grouse hawking for that day was a non-starter. And the member of our party who was most disappointed was the keeper. He asked if the little tiercel, or 'wee little man' as he called him, would fly anything else other than game. I explained that in our early days together he had flown and caught a lot of starlings and the keeper immediately perked up and set off across the moor at a cracking pace. We eventually reached a rocky gorge that had plenty of rowan trees in the bottom.

Shakey was put on the wing and allowed to cruise around. With there being no dog on point he did not make any height, but he did stay above the gorge as we ran down it trying to flush small birds for him to chase. The keeper was getting so excited he was even throwing his hat at the trees to get the starlings to shift. What a turnaround from someone who had been so completely disinterested in the sport of falconry on our arrival. When our stay finally came to an end the keeper declared that he thought Shakey a 'bonnie wee hawk' and that he would always be welcome on his ground. Since this time the keeper and I have become very firm friends and we have enjoyed a great many days' sport together.

On several occasions, usually late on in the grouse season when at the peak of his fitness, Shakey would literally go up out of sight in a clear blue sky. The only way that we, down on the ground, would know when he was overhead, and the moment to flush was right, was by using the telemetry. But although the stoop produced in these flights was truly spectacular they rarely ended in success. It would always take Shakey too long to get down and get on terms with the grouse. They would have plenty of warning and would put in before any real danger overtook them. But the stoops really were spectacular to watch.

In Shakey's final season with me a journalist made last minute arrangements to come out with us and see some grouse hawking. The weather was very hit and miss, one of those days when one minute it is pouring with rain and the next the sun is out and shining brightly. We made our way onto the moor and eventually got a good point in a favourable location for our purposes. But it was going to be a now or never action as storm clouds were rapidly gathering. Shakey duly took to the air and mounted nicely above the dogs. The journalist asked where the best place to stand was so that he could see all the flight and get some decent photographs. I pointed out what I considered to be a likely spot, although there are never any guarantees, and got on with heading the point. When all was set fair the dogs were sent in to flush and a lovely flight and stoop ensued. The grouse was hit fair and square and literally dropped less than a dozen feet away from our guest.

He was very excited and expressed all the normal views about the grace and power of the falcon and what a good and fair field sport falconry is. I commented that his positioning could not have been better for his photography. The shots he got should have been first rate and I enquired as to whether or not there would be any chance of buying some from him. It turned out that he had become so excited he had totally forgotten to take any pictures. What a waste! But then I know how easy it is to get carried away in such a situation; I have done it often enough myself.

One of the joys with flying Shakey was the way he obviously revelled in his own flying prowess. On many occasions when waiting on in anticipation of a grouse being flushed a small bird would be disturbed into taking flight by the action of the falconers heading the point. Often as not, Shakey would stoop at these and take them with ease. Having caught and killed them he would then drop them and go back up to wait on again in expectation of his grouse. I am sure that he also killed sometimes out of sheer frustration and temper. I well remember an instance when he missed a partridge and on his way back he suddenly veered off and flew down and killed a rook. Having despatched the rook he then came straight back into the lure. A rook is a formidable quarry for a full size peregrine falcon, which is more than double Shakey's size.

Another of this little falcon's remarkable traits was to come back looking for me when he had a full crop. This was extremely useful on occasions when he had killed out of sight and I had failed to track him down. In most cases of this sort the result would be a lost falcon. But Shakey would appear from nowhere and come sailing in and land at my feet. He would then step up on the glove without being offered any food. To do so would have proved futile as his crop was always already bulging to bursting point. All in all he performed this little trick about a dozen times in our career together.

Shakey also had some strange little ways that were not quite so endearing. For example, whenever I went to pick him up off his block he would bate away from me. But I very soon learnt that if he bated once, then got straight back on his block and from there jumped to the fist, he was ready to fly. If he bated twice he was definitely not ready. Of course when friends saw me pick him up to fly and he bated away from me they were sure that the day was doomed to failure and I must be crazy to fly him. He also hated to be touched. During his initial manning process I had done all the normal things a falconer is supposed to do, stroking him with a feather to start with and then, when he would accept this, gradually substituting the hand. For the first season this was fine. I could do whatever I wanted. But from the start of the second season this was definitely not on. He would bite or foot me if I even tried to touch him, yet he had never been handled roughly or given any reason to resent being touched. I think as his confidence grew in his own abilities he failed to see any reason why he should be handled more than was absolutely necessary. Yet he would let me clean his beak and talons for him after a kill. Once cleaned, though, he would bite me if I tried to touch him again.

Even though I never get tired of singing the praises of this little falcon he did, on occasions, let me down. I had an invitation to go grouse hawking with a falconer I have admired and respected for thirty years or so. I wanted everything to go well and let him see just how good this falcon was. Accordingly, I got up very early on the day in question and put Shakey out to have a bath so that he would be dry in plenty of time for the day's sport. He always appreciated the opportunity to have a bath before flying and if I was lax in offering it he would go off and find a suitable puddle for himself. On this special day he was straight in, despite the earliness of the hour, and had a thoroughly good time. It didn't take long for him to dry off and he was soon fully ready to give a good account of himself in the field.

The car was loaded up and we set off for the short drive to the destination for the day. My host is renowned for his generosity and accordingly gave me first flight. This had no sooner been agreed than the brace of pointers he was running came on a staunch point. Off came Shakey's hood and jesses and he was in the air. But not for long. He started to mount well enough and then put in a shallow stoop and was lost from sight. Our host was excited and remarked that a lot of snipe had arrived on the moor and perhaps he had spotted one and taken it. But no, I found him wallowing in a peat hag that was filled with disgusting brown water. I felt extremely embarrassed and apologised to my host for wasting the point, but I was at pains to point out that Shakey had already bathed before setting off from home. My host said not to worry, these things happen, and he would fly the point. His tiercel peregrine was soon in the air and starting to climb nicely. Then it too peeled off and sat on a rock, where it stayed despite all offerings and temptations for the next twenty minutes. Bad luck for my host, but it did make me feel considerably better. It shows that we are all fallible.

Generally speaking, though, Shakey could be relied upon if guests were joining us for some sport. He would fly with style and put on a creditable performance. He has given considerable pleasure to many and I am sure he will be remembered fondly by all those who've been fortunate enough to see him fly. Shakey and I had very many good experiences together and shared some wonderful sport. He may have been extremely small but he made up for his lack of stature by having a heart as big as a lion. He even repeated his trick of taking two grouse out of the same covey once more in his career. As it happened it was in front of a group of falconers who'd doubted if he was capable of taking a grouse at all. But the most important thing about Shakey was his style, for he was always a high mounter and deadly accurate in the stoop.

I am flying his sister now and she is a great deal of fun. But Laina, as of yet, has not come up to the standard set by Shakey. She did kill the first ever grouse that was flushed under her, but it took her a long time to get her second. Laina tries hard and flies nicely but she does not have the style and dash of Shakey. I doubt if I will ever have another falcon that will. No falconer gets two hawks like this in a lifetime.

CHAPTER FOUR

# Bubble and Squeak

BUBBLE and Squeak are two North American prairie falcons that had an extremely miserable start to their lives. Fortunately circumstances altered and they were able to enjoy many happy years doing what nature had originally intended them for. When I took over the presentation and running of the bird of prey flying displays at Windsor Safari Park, Bubble and Squeak had been in residence there for about twelve weeks. They had come to Windsor by a very indirect route. Originally captive bred in Canada, they had been sold to a dealer on the continent. He had then sold them to a safari park in Holland. Windsor wanted to buy several birds of prey from the park in Holland and the two prairie falcons became part of the deal. The Dutch wanted rid of them and Windsor didn't really want them either, but to obtain what they did want, a bald eagle and a turkey vulture, they had to agree to purchase the prairies.

The reason that no one was over-keen to have the prairies was that they were imprinted falcons and therefore noisy and extremely aggressive. Prairie falcons are aggressive by nature anyway and two malimprinted specimens were just not desirable. Social imprints are a totally different thing, pleasant to fly and good mannered, but malimprints are generally pretty horrible. On their arrival in England they were placed in quarantine for thirty-five days and after this they were put into weatherings and just thrown food while it was decided what should be done with them. When I took over, the prairies were in a pitiful state. They had been just left to their own devices day in and day out so their plumage and equipment were in a dreadful state. Their jesses were literally as stiff as cardboard and matted together with their own droppings.

When I was being shown round by my new employers I saw the prairies being fed. They were both thrown a split rabbit's head and left to get on with it. When their weatherings were being cleaned out, apparently, they were held at leash length with the aid of a broom. No wonder these two falcons were aggressive and not overly fond of humans. I was informed that the make-up of the display team would be left in my hands and I could get rid of these two problem falcons just as soon as I liked. The thought of them being passed from pillar to post for the rest of their lives was one that I couldn't live with. I decided there and then to get these two falcons flying properly so that they could enjoy life instead of being tied to blocks all the time. To see any bird or animal being treated in this way is upsetting. I have always had a soft spot for prairie falcons so I was doubly determined to do well by them.

None of the members of the human team I had inherited wanted to touch the falcons at all, so instead of changing the falcons I changed the humans. I wanted people with me who were enthusiastic and eager to fly falcons, not content with just throwing them food. Two full-time replacements were duly found, along with a couple of part-timers, and while they concentrated on the day-to-day work I made a start on the two prairies.

The first job was to get them fitted with some new equipment and weigh them so as to give me a reference point for training. New jesses, swivels and leashes were fitted and a decent pair of hoods sorted out. Beaks and talons were trimmed and some minor imping carried out. While they had been left in their weatherings they had rubbed the tips off their primary wing feathers. An assortment of peregrine falcon feathers did the trick and at least they now looked like working falcons. Because of their vocal nature the names Bubble and Squeak suggested themselves. Bubble was the slightly smaller of the two and Squeak was certainly the more aggressive. She was not scared of anyone or anything. Both falcons weighed well over two pounds and were as fat as butter, so a reduction in weight was going to be required before any progress could be made. But from the moment the equipment was changed I wanted to move gradually forward with them. I would only let them feed on the fist and to ensure that they could eat quantity but still lose weight I fed them washed rabbit meat. This meant they could eat three-quarter crops of food each day but still actually lose weight at an acceptable rate.

I spent as much time as I could with each falcon on the fist during the day, initially hooded most of the time but as their weight came down then the hoods were removed for longer and longer periods. Meal times became less of a battle of wills and more of a pleasant interlude. As Squeak approached the one pound thirteen ounce mark a change came over her general demeanour. Instead of bating away at my approach she would actually step up onto the fist and look for food. Previously, when I had managed to finally get her up onto the fist, she would lie along my arm and bite my upper arm as hard as she could, beating her wings to keep her balance. It was a thoroughly nasty and painful experience. With patience and perseverance, though, I was definitely starting to win. Hooding her was still a major battle each time but this was something that just had to be done.

Once the initial barriers had been broken down progress started to be made at a relatively rapid rate. Squeak started to jump to the fist and was soon introduced to the lure. She was very unsure of it at first and it took a long time to click with her that the lure's production meant food for her. But with repetition the lesson was eventually learnt. It had to be remembered all the time that these falcons had been mistreated originally so their view of humans and their resulting behaviour was a prejudiced one. Only patience and lots of care was going to win them over. Once Squeak associated the lure with food she came to it instantly whenever it was produced. Squeak was as ready as she was ever going to be to be flown loose.

The first time loose she was called off and when she was on her way the lure was hidden from sight. Squeak flew round me and then I threw the lure out on the ground. She came straight in to it without any hesitation. She was allowed to take a good meal from the lure and then taken back up on the fist. Despite her awful start in life her manners were relatively good and she willingly took titbits from the fingers. Occasionally she took them out of the fingers as well, but I think this was more an imprint's desperate need for food as opposed to being outright malicious and deliberately trying to bite me. Progress continued at a steady rate and by day five she was circling well and then putting in a couple of stoops. Obviously it was going to take a considerable while to get her fit enough to go into display but I was pleased with what we had done so far.

On day six a problem manifested itself that was never to be overcome, despite lots of work and patience. I assume it was a result of her poor treatment earlier in life, but Squeak would not allow anyone else near her when she was on the lure. On the day in question I had flown her and called her down to the lure as normal. I was kneeling beside her giving her titbits as she ate and quietly talking to her when a work colleague came over to tell me I was wanted on the telephone. As he got within a few yards Squeak's neck feathers stood out and she adopted a very aggressive posture. I suggested that my colleague stop where he was for a moment until I had picked her up, but he continued coming towards me, saying 'It's only a falcon.' As soon as he was close to me Squeak left the lure and flew up onto his head. She clawed and bit him for a few moments and then returned to her lure. In just a few short seconds she had inflicted a lot of damage, for blood was oozing from various points on his head and neck. Back on the lure Squeak was still displaying her threat mode. As he backed off she calmly shook her feathers into place and started to feed again as if nothing had happened.

Having finished her meal she stepped up onto the fist as if butter wouldn't melt in her mouth. Once her leash and swivel were safely back in place and she was well and truly secured to my glove my colleague approached again. Squeak did not take the slightest bit of notice of him. Subsequently she made her threat displays several more times to other people – but only when she was on the lure. It would appear that she trusted me and would tolerate me near at hand while she fed, but no one else. At the time, however, this was not the conclusion that I drew. I put it down to the fact that she would not tolerate two people close at hand. Now as Squeak was going to be used for displays it was important that more than one person should be able to handle her and fly her. Having talked the situation over with my staff it was decided that the following day one of the others would fly her. All went well initially. Squeak allowed herself to be picked up, hooded and weighed all without any show of tantrum. When she was cast off she circled round as normal and did several passes to the lure when asked. The lure was thrown out and down she came upon it. The assistant who had flown her started to make into her and she immediately adopted her threat posture. I called out not to go any closer and that I would make in and pick her up. The assistant maintained that he was sure that if he kept offering her titbits everything would be all right. As he leaned forward to give her a tasty morsel Squeak flew at him and attached herself to his neck. She was clawing and biting for all she was worth. But to give my assistant his due he drew his arms up to protect his face and called out for me to get her off as quickly as possible. I ran over and as I neared her Squeak gave a little chup and jumped back on her lure. I then picked her up and she totally ignored the assistant. I remarked to my assistant that I was very pleased that he hadn't tried to brush Squeak off by using physical force and he said that after the sort of start she had had in life she deserved better. This was something I always admired him for and in later life was more than happy to give him a helping hand when he needed one.

But by now the problem was obvious; the falcon trusted me and no one else, which meant that on my days off Squeak could not be flown at the park. This was an inconvenience as opposed to a major problem and it meant that I exercised Squeak at home on such occasions.

Bubble was a week or so behind Squeak in her training as she had an awful fear of getting up onto the glove. Every time the free hand came into sight she would throw herself off the fist in a mad panic. It was obvious that she had been struck by someone prior to coming to us.

It makes one wonder as to the mentality of a person who could strike a falcon, weighing around two pounds, purely because it annoyed them for a moment or two. I once had the misfortune to work with a so-called falconer who always said that if a hawk or falcon played him up he gave them the helicopter treatment and it did them the world of good. I didn't know what this meant until one day a hawk bated constantly off his fist and he treated it to a session of being whirled around and around by its jesses. I left immediately.

It took a tremendous amount of work to get Bubble over her fear of the ungloved hand and to regain her confidence. I went about it by feeding her juicy titbits from the fingers of my free hand, deliberately making every movement very slowly and carefully. The situation did get better but she never fully overcame her fear. If I were to forget and try to do something with my free hand at a normal pace she would bate off the fist instantly. But providing I remembered to move slowly then at least I could make progress with her.

Bubble was flown loose without the accompanying traumas that Squeak gave us. She took even longer to get fit and for the first few days could only just skim over the grass and would land on the lure, panting for all she was worth. But after a month or so both prairies were flying well and were on the wing for a considerable time. Squeak, despite her peculiarities, was the better flyer of the two and would go up to very good heights and then come in and put on a tremendous display of stooping. She was obviously going to be a real crowd pleaser. Bubble was going to be more of a steady work horse, not doing anything spectacular but putting on a reliable performance.

The public shows were due to start at Windsor on the Easter weekend, and here we were six weeks ahead of schedule with both falcons flying well. The park used to be full of rooks and crows and this became too much for me to ignore. After all, I was a falconer first and foremost. I switched flying both falcons to a dead rook as a lure. Squeak accepted the change immediately but Bubble took several days before she would willingly come down on it. When both would come immediately to the new lure I gave them short rations early one day with the hope of trying to catch a corvid the next.

Windsor Safari Park was not ideal for flying rooks and crows, in that it was a typical piece of English parkland, with plenty of trees amid open grassy areas. But I thought that, even if the circumstances were against us, we would give it a go. Prairies also have a reputation for following quarry into cover so perhaps the trees would not ruin all the flights. Bubble was the first to have a go, and although she took off after a small group she was unhooded at, she didn't really fly them with gusto. As the rooks put into the trees Bubble peeled off and came back, looking for the lure. She needed to be a little keener and was given her day's rations there and then and put away in readiness for the next day.

Squeak had a totally different attitude. She was off the fist like a rocket and, as the rooks put into a large oak tree, she was straight in among them and grabbed one. The two of them tumbled to earth and the struggle was very soon over. I do admit to wondering what her reaction was going to be towards me as I approached her on the kill. After the episodes with the lure I went towards her with a great deal of caution, mentally preparing myself for a display of temper and some lacerations. But I need not have worried. She was her normal calm self with me and I helped her break into her rook and feed up on it.

Squeak went on to catch many more rooks and we had to develop many different tactics to be able to get a flight at them at all, for they soon got used to our vehicle and us. As soon as we appeared they were off. We overcame this problem by spotting groups of rooks out feeding with binoculars. Then we would go off half a mile or so in the opposite direction. Once well and truly out of sight of the rooks, Squeak would be put on the wing. She would circle around for a while staying relatively close, and would then start to gain some height – not a tremendous pitch, but certainly two hundred feet or so. Once she was up to this sort of height I would walk forward and bring her over the rooks feeding on the ground.

We always reached a point of no return with this method. The rooks would, as often as not, spot Squeak working her way up, but because she did not offer an immediate threat to them they would carry on feeding. Then, when I started to walk forward, Squeak would be getting closer to them, but her height often acted as a deterrent to their making a bolt for it. This was the tricky part. Once we got within a few hundred yards of them they were committed to staying. Then a good flight and stoop would ensue. Sometimes the whole procedure fell apart and the rooks would take flight the minute they saw the falcon's silhouette in the sky. Squeak would still give chase but it was normally a futile exercise.

This method of flying gradually taught Squeak to get much higher very quickly, something that was to prove excellent in her display work at a later date. We had a few good weeks of sport and accounted for a decent number of corvids. It may not have been falconry in the grand style, but at least we were hunting daily and catching quarry. Bubble did catch a few rooks, having dropped her weight a little more, but she never flew them with gusto and would give up the flight at the least excuse. Her character had mellowed a little and now other people could fly her as long as they were slow and deliberate in their movements around her. Even so, I was extremely happy that the two sad and sorry falcons I had first seen were now both flying free and doing what nature intended them to do.

All too soon the display season was on us and that put an end to the hunting flights. Or at least it should have done. Both falcons were raised in weight as they did not need to be so keen to fly a lure as they did to fly quarry. This raising of the weight should have meant that they did not have the stimulation to want to work hard to achieve a kill. Windsor used to attract vast crowds and the flying displays on a bank holiday would produce an audience of several thousand. Squeak revelled in the fact that she had an audience. When she came in to stoop to the lure she would use the crowd as a screen to try and sneak up on me, flying behind a group of people and then suddenly flipping up over the top of them. She would even fly between people's legs. All too soon she was a celebrity and people would come and time again just to see her fly. As her confidence grew she developed a party piece all of her own.

When she was released from the fist she would power off in a straight line as far as the eye could see. Needless to say the audience thought that she had gone. We would carry on with the display and fly a barn owl to the fist for several minutes. When we had finished with the barn owl we would ask the audience if they thought that Squeak was going to come back. The answer was nearly always a mumbled no, accompanied by a shaking of heads. Then I would point out that if they would all like to look upwards they would see Squeak circling high above them. She would be a tiny dot in the sky directly over the arena. I would then produce the lure and give a yell and Squeak would fold her wings and come in.

She would then put on a display of stooping that was second to none. She would always draw thunderous applause and the public grew to love her – most of the public, that is. Squeak had not forgotten her hunting experiences and several times blotted her copy book during a display. Because she used to go off for up to ten minutes to gain height before coming back over the arena, the local bird life used to make the false assumption it was safe. Every now and again a rook would flap its way slowly across the flying arena. If Squeak was in effective range then as often as not this would be the rook's last ever journey. Several times she stooped and knocked a rook down into the arena during a display. She nearly always killed them outright so no great harm was done as far as the public were concerned, but on one occasion she hit one and knocked it to the ground where it was very definitely still alive and kicking. Squeak came down on it and a massive tussle ensued. When Squeak had finally subdued and despatched the rook I thought there might be problems with the audience, but when I explained what had happened a great cheer went up.

I only ever experienced one extremely irate gentleman as a result of Squeak's flying prowess. He and his family were enjoying a picnic on the grass adjacent to the flying arena. Squeak knocked down and killed a rook which landed literally in the middle of the neatly laid out feast. Because of the close proximity of the family Squeak would not come down on her kill but kept circling and calling all the time. I went over and picked the rook up and brought Squeak down to the lure. The man was absolutely livid and demanded that I pay for him and his family to have another lunch. I refused and he stormed to the administration building, demanding to see a superior. The administration did actually give him and his family lunch.

Bubble was far better behaved and performed her daily stints with clockwork reliability. She was used for some television work and became quite a firm favourite with the public. But she never had the fire that Squeak did.

Circumstances changed at Windsor and I left to pursue other avenues. I tried very hard to buy Bubble and Squeak but the administration would have none of it. Bubble could be flown by anyone but Squeak was useless to them as only I could handle or fly her. But they would not sell them, believing that both falcons would fly just as well for someone else. Apparently Squeak was flown once by my replacement and the lacerations received on this one occasion were enough to convince him that he would never fly her again. So this magnificent falcon went back to being stuck in a weathering and thrown food without the prospect of flying loose again.

Not too long after my departure the safari park hit trouble and was sold off. I asked a friend to make an approach and purchase Bubble and Squeak on my behalf. He had seen both falcons fly many times and wanted Bubble for himself, an arrangement which suited both of us admirably. The last I heard Bubble was thirteen years old and still flying as well as ever.

Squeak came back to me and I like to think that we were both very happy about it. However, one trait of her character that had never manifested itself before now rose to the surface. Squeak hated women. If my wife or mother showed themselves in the garden while she was out weathering, Squeak would go mad. She would call and bate at them as if possessed. Should one of them make the mistake of walking too close to her they would very soon find an irate prairie falcon attached to the back of their legs.

Squeak and I immediately made a start on getting to know each other properly again and very soon I had her full confidence once more. In the period when we were apart Squeak had lost two toes off one foot. I don't know how this happened, and I doubt that I ever will, but I do have my suspicions. Within ten days Squeak was flying at the lure with all her old gusto and was ready to start rook hawking again. She was straight back into her stride and killed the second time of asking. And now we were away from the park and its natural confines we were able to carry out rook hawking with much more style. Open countryside was where we hunted and the flights accordingly were much longer and far more enjoyable. Squeak had time to fetch her rooks properly and would now stoop at them and strike them, as opposed to just grabbing them. Her score mounted steadily and she became so proficient that we would go out with the intention of catching two a day.

Normally I feed a falcon up when it has made a kill, so that it always believes the effort was worthwhile and continues to fly quarry with gusto. But often when Squeak caught a rook with her first flight you could sense that she was still keen and absolutely full of flying, so I started flying her twice instead of just the once. In fact, to be perfectly honest, the first time I flew her twice on the same day was her decision not mine. We had an invitation from a friend to join him rook hawking on Salisbury Plain. Squeak had flown and caught her rook and I was in the process of making slowly in to her. Three or four rooks were wheeling round overhead, cawing and generally showing their displeasure at the demise of one of their brethren. Squeak had despatched her rook and was starting to plume the carcass ready to eat it. Each time the rooks circled over her she would stop what she was doing and look up at them. Eventually it all got too much for her and she left her meal and took to the air in pursuit of her tormentors.

Because the rooks were already above her they relied on the fact that they could stay above her to keep out of trouble. They were wrong. Squeak worked for all she was worth to get on terms with them. When she eventually achieved this the rooks took flight downwind at a terrific pace. But Squeak was up to the chase and knocked one down about three-quarters of a mile away from us. We ran after her for all we were worth and discovered her happily tucking in to kill number two. This time the rooks did not come back to mob her.

She also killed a great number of magpies when we were out hawking. Magpies, being cunning creatures, would spot Squeak and dive into the nearest bush believing that they were completely safe. In fact once in the bush the normal thing was for the magpie to flick its tail and repeatedly utter its displeasure vocally. The problem for the magpies was that no one had ever bothered to explain to Squeak that falcons do not enter cover after their prey. As soon as the magpie started to call, from what it considered the safety of a bush or small tree, Squeak would simply crash in after it. They were never very sporting flights, certainly not from the magpie's point of view anyway. The strange thing was that, having killed a magpie, she would then ignore it. She certainly had no desire to eat one. I suppose her red letter day as far as magpies were concerned was when she killed two together. I had spotted a family party of seven out feeding together. I slipped Squeak at them and they duly headed for the nearest bush, which happened to be a blackthorn. The magpies settled in the top and started to cackle at the falcon and flick their tails. Squeak, as per normal, piled straight into them and fell to the ground clutching one in each foot.

I had tremendous fun flying Squeak and was really happy with her, but she did take up an awful amount of my time. An old friend, Roger Weeks, came over to visit one Sunday afternoon. Squeak was out on the lawn weathering and Roger remarked what a good looking falcon she was. He knew her full history and had always followed her career with interest. He was without a falcon at the time so I asked him, rather on the spur of the moment, if he would like to take over flying her. It was a decision I was never even momentarily to regret. I knew that he had the patience to help Squeak make the transition from one falconer to another and he was certainly skilled enough to do her justice when it came to flying. So Squeak went home with Roger, on the understanding that if for any reason they did not get on, he would bring her back.

Squeak and Roger got on well enough, after one or two little initial traumas. They enjoyed a good career together and Roger even brought her to Scotland one season to give her a crack at grouse. It was particularly nice for me to see her again flying quarry at close quarters. Despite her time with Roger she definitely remembered me and allowed me to pick her up and handle her as I had always done.

Squeak is retired from flying now and is happily turning out young falcons, by means of artificial insemination, so at least her progeny will be flying quarry in the hands of falconers for many years to come. When I think back to the state, both mental and physical, she was in when I first saw her I am very happy that we had the time together that we did.

CHAPTER FIVE

# The American
# Air Force falcons

WHEN I was a great deal younger, far more idealistic and with fewer commitments, I spent several years doing bird control work with trained falcons. At the time there were several firms who had obtained various contracts to clear rubbish tips, military bases and such like of unwanted avian visitors by means of trained falcons. One of the firms in this field had a series of contracts with the American Air Force to keep bases they were using over here free from birds. This is because a bird strike, as a collision between a bird and an aircraft is known, can prove extremely costly and sometimes fatal.

The time of maximum risk to aircraft is takeoff and landing. Airfields, by their very nature, are ideal feeding grounds for birds and therefore attract very large numbers of them. One of the most effective ways of persuading the avian visitors to move on is by constantly flying falcons over the territory they would like to feed on. Many other methods of bird control have been tried, ranging from the bizarre to the thoroughly ridiculous. But falcons, being natural predators, get the job done and done well. That does mean, though, that falcons must be flown regularly throughout the hours of daylight, day in, day out, to convince the local bird population that this is not a good place to risk feeding.

Some of the people who went into this line of work fooled themselves that they were being professional falconers, but of course they were not. Falconry is the sport of catching live quarry in its natural environment with a trained hawk or falcon. In bird control work, to kill is the last thing you want to achieve. After all, the falcon is effective because it represents a risk to the feeding birds, who therefore move on rather than risk being killed. If the falcon were to kill then the rest of the birds would think that it was now okay to carry on feeding, so falcons, particularly lanners and luggers, were encouraged to soar or stoop repeatedly to the lure.

Although falcons were being flown on a daily basis, they were certainly not being used for falconry. But if you could accept that fact then it did mean you had the opportunity to do nothing else except train and fly falcons day in and day out. I went to work for a firm that had the bird clearance contract for a few USAF air bases in East Anglia. Although my day-to-day job was not falconry it did give me the opportunity to be surrounded by falcons and have nothing else to do but look after their needs and train and fly them.

The basic brief for the work was that falcons would be flown every hour or so, regardless of whether birds were on the airfield or not. In this way it was hoped to establish in the minds of the local resident bird population that this was too dangerous a place to be. We also had two-way radio communication with the control tower. If they spotted any birds within the vicinity of the airfield they would contact us. A falcon would then be readied and flown to shift the unwelcome guests. It was a system that seemed to work well. There were certainly no bird strikes recorded while falcons were being employed at these airfields.

If you were young and still fairly uncommitted it was one of those jobs that meant you were left alone to get on with things. Providing the airfield was kept clear everybody was happy. Once the initial hard work had been put in then the job itself was extremely easy and straightforward. In the early days falcons were flown literally every half-hour or so to ensure a more or less constant presence. The falcons, coupled with flares and taped distress calls, soon had the area relatively free of unwanted visitors. Once the breeding season was underway most birds that would have taken up residence on the base and fed on it had made their homes elsewhere. So after a period of about six weeks of very intensive flying things became a lot calmer and a lot easier.

It then meant that the falconers employed on the bases could fly what they wanted and when as opposed to having to follow a strict regime. The down side to the job was that it was a dawn till dusk operation seven days a week. But at the start of each week the control tower would send down a list of weekly aircraft movement and it was possible to plan around this. Exceptions were visiting NATO aircraft, but we nearly always received at least one hour's warning of their arrival. When we knew something was due to land or take off we would have a quick drive round the base to ensure that it was bird free.

Each base actually had two falconers allocated to it and it was pretty important that the pair got on together. After all, they spent more time in each other's company than the average married couple. Some of the bases had excellent living conditions and some were exceedingly poor. The base where I spent the majority of my time had a superb mews and kennel arrangements for the falcons and dogs. The human living conditions, on the other hand, were absolutely diabolical. But because I and the person working with me were happy flying our falcons all day we put up with it.

As I am sure most people are aware these air bases, be they British or American, are very self-contained. We had plenty of places where we could eat and several alternatives for evening entertainment. However, we had our own entertainment laid on for most evenings: the base was alive with rabbits, which came out to feed mainly at night. Accordingly I bought for myself a beautiful lurcher dog called Trampass, a deerhound cross greyhound who took his looks from the deerhound side of the cross. We used to run him at the rabbits at night in the lights of the car. He would catch sufficient rabbits to feed himself, the hawks and on occasion us. Indeed, he was so keen that the major problem we had was stopping him running.

At the time the vehicles we used for patrolling the base were a pair of mini vans. They were cheap, easy to repair and convenient for putting hawks and dogs in the back. The major drawback was that they had sliding windows in the front. We would be driving along, looking to pick up rabbits in the headlights, and the dog would be standing up looking out between our shoulders. As the headlights picked up a rabbit he would try and launch himself out through the silly little windows with their tiny aperture. How he never hurt himself seriously I will never know. We tried rigging up a screen between front and back but nothing ever worked. Trampass would merely pull it down till he could see out again.

For obvious reasons we would always inform the base security police before venturing out to hunt. Sometimes the security patrols would follow us to see what it was we were doing. Several of the guards came to enjoy the coursing and it ended so that we had to draw up a rota for those who wanted to accompany us. These same guards would call round and see us during the day and bring bones and scraps of meat for the lurcher. I swear he lived a great deal better than we did.

Several of them also took an interest in the falcons and would make a point of coming to see them fly. We had many incidents during our time on the base and most can be looked back on with fondness. I had heard of falconers on other bases having terrible accidents with their falcons, mainly flying into things and killing themselves. But fortunately nothing like that ever happened to us. We certainly had a few mishaps, but happily ours tended to be of a comical nature.

This work took place in the days when you could still import passage and haggard falcons from abroad. The majority of falcons used for this type of work were lanners, because they were relatively easy to obtain and train, and because of their tendency to go on the soar. Being flown in such open spaces, and with the thermals that the large expanses of concrete give off, it was very easy to get a lanner or lanneret to go right up almost out of sight on a clear day. For the falconer this is a sheer pleasure to watch and from a bird control point of view very effective. Obviously birds are reluctant to move under a falcon at such a tremendous height. As we were young we used to fool ourselves that these lanners were waiting on, but of course they were doing nothing of the kind. They were simply soaring round and enjoying themselves. This is easy enough to prove. If you throw a lure out and give the normal shout that the falcon would associate with feeding, it should come in instantly. But what used to happen in actual fact was that the falcon

*A hooded female red headed merlin – the same breed as the author's first bird, Remus*

*Falconer Andy Gibbs with Dawn, the peregrine falcon*

*Dawn, on the lure*

*A young peregrine falcon*

*Shakey, the tiercel red naped shaheen, on a grouse (third season)*

*Shakey in his fourth season*

*The author with a cast of red shaheens*

*Shakey's sister, Laina, a red naped shaheen*

*A kestrel. The author trained and then released an injured kestrel during his time working on bird control for the American Airforce*

*A saker, one of the types of falcon the author used for bird clearance work during his time in Austria*

*An adult female goshawk such as the one the author flew while in Austria*

# A SELECTION
# OF THE TYPES OF HAWK AND FALCON
# THE AUTHOR HAS SEEN DURING HIS TRAVELS
# IN NORTH AMERICA

*An adult red tail hawk*

*A bald eagle*

*A male Harris' hawk*

*A white gyr falcon*

*A grey phase gyr falcon*

*A female gyr/prairie falcon*

*A female gyr/saker falcon*

*Cerri Griffiths, from the
Welsh Hawking Centre,
casting off a gyr hybrid*

*A male gyr/peregrine hybrid*

*The author with a gyr/peregrine hybrid*

*A peregrine/lanner hybrid*

*A perlin – a peregrine/merlin hybrid*

*A Barbary falcon at
12 weeks old*

*An adult Barbary falcon*

*A tawny eagle*

*Evie and Emma, the pointers*

*Evie and a gyr/peregrine hybrid on a grouse he has just killed*

*Evie and Emma flushing grouse for a shooting party*

*A goshawk on a rabbit. This picture was taken during one of the author's hawking trips to Scotland*

*One-week-old home-bred peregrine falcons being fed.
The author plans to move to Scotland and fly peregrine
falcons that he has bred and hacked himself.*

*The author's hawking cottage in Scotland*

would come in when it felt like it. Sometimes it would be immediately, sometimes an hour later. But the falcons were enjoying themselves and we were enjoying them.

Several of the birds we flew developed into real characters. We had a male lugger falcon that had been imported from India in adult plumage. This haggard lugger was very crafty when he flew. After all, he had spent several years in the wild coping quite nicely for himself. He would not go up on the soar at any price. No matter how hard we tried and however fit we got him, he would not go above forty feet or so. What he would do was hunt jackdaws and magpies with a vengeance. Life in the wild had obviously taught him the best technique for hunting these species and he applied it very successfully when he was with us. He was flown by either me or the friend working with me, as we wanted him to fly every day without a miss. We would employ the normal tactics for hunting corvids, that is, we would select a group that were out upwind of us so when the falcon took off from the fist it was flying directly into the wind. In this way it could use its superior flying powers to cut into the wind and make ground on its quarry. When looking for a slip of this type it is important that you are at least half the distance from your intended quarry as they are themselves from cover. This means that if you are a hundred and fifty yards from your quarry when you slip the falcon, the nearest upwind cover should be three hundred yards from them. In the classic flight the falcon will make towards its quarry, gaining in height as it flies into the wind. By the time it reaches them it will be well above them and in a position to put in a stoop.

What our little lugger used to do was to flap along just above the ground. He would also fly so slowly that he gave the impression he was going to land any minute. Occasionally the quarry would take off as soon as they spotted him, flying off into the blue yonder and heading for safety. But nine times out of ten, because the falcon did not look like it was flying in earnest, they would merely lift up and down and generally be a little restless. As the lugger got closer they would lift up and circle round at about twenty feet or so. Instead of taking flight they would actually start cawing and mobbing the little falcon. The lugger would ignore them and pass beneath them, carrying on as if heading into the distance. Once the corvids came back down again he would suddenly turn and accelerate hard into them. This tactic nearly always paid off and he would grab a jackdaw as it rose. It didn't matter where we flew the lugger, he would always employ the same tricks.

Magpies were another victim that he outfoxed on a regular basis, but these he would handle in a slightly different way. Again he would fly towards them slowly and deliberately, but the magpies would take off and go and sit in the nearest piece of cover, be it a tree or a bush. The lugger would fly past them into the next piece of cover. He would then sit disinterestedly and start to preen his feathers. After a while the magpies would come across and start to mob him. He would ignore them and let them get bolder and bolder. Sooner or later one would forget itself and, in his efforts to mob the falcon, would fly past the falcon on the wrong side with regard to its original cover. The moment the magpie was in this position the lugger was out and after it for all he was worth. It was a method that rarely failed and only nature could have taught the lugger. What did amaze me was that this ploy would work more than once against the same group of magpies. Providing you didn't try and hunt the same group too often it still worked, despite the fact that the group would already have witnessed one of their number being caught in this fashion.

It was always amusing when we had friends out with us who had specifically come to see the lugger fly. We would tell them that he was excellent at catching jackdaws and magpies and no one believed us, so they would come out to see for themselves. What we didn't do was tell them how he did it. Of course when the lugger left the fist and employed his 'stealth is the best policy' approach, you could see them thinking that this was going to be a waste of time. Then, when he caught one, they had to change their minds. This little lugger was the only falcon I have ever had that could catch jackdaws. Normally they are far too agile and clever to be caught.

The bird control on the base was so effective that we did not often get the opportunity to fly the lugger at quarry within the confines of the airfield, although on two occasions we did fly him at jackdaws. Both flights ended in chaos for others. The first was when he employed his normal trick of attacking a jackdaw and the flight ended inside a hangar where two McDonnel Douglas F4 Phantoms were undergoing routine maintenance. Not only that, but the battle actually ended on the pilot's seat of one of the aircraft. I was in hot pursuit of both lugger and jackdaw as they entered the hangar and it was amazing to see the chaos and panic that two relatively small birds could create in just a few seconds. But that was not all. This hangar was a restricted area as far as non-airforce personnel were concerned. The armed guards on the hangar doors would not let me enter and retrieve the falcon until they had cleared it on the radio with their superiors. Only then was I allowed to collect my falcon and his meal under the eyes of a guard armed with an M16 armalite rifle – apparently this was in case ! decided suddenly to steal a plane.

The other flight ended even more chaotically. The jackdaw, in its efforts to throw off the hard pressing falcon, had taken to flying in between a series of buildings, one of which was the base mess hall. This building seated about two thousand people at lunch time and the flow of human traffic through the twin doors was constant. The jackdaw, in a last ditch attempt to throw off the lugger, flew between the doors and into the mess hall. The lugger, not to be deterred, chased straight on in after it. From the noise emitting from the hall you would think a full-scale riot had broken out. The lugger had caught its prey more or less in the middle of the hall. As I entered the hall I knew exactly where he was by the crowd that had gathered round him, so I retrieved him as quickly as possible and made a hasty exit. A few days later I received a memo from the base commander. It stated quite clearly that although the falconers were allowed to partake of meals in the mess hall their falcons definitely were not. In future would we please ensure they stayed out of any base eating facilities. Apparently this memo was not meant to be tongue in cheek, but in earnest.

When winter came to the base life changed completely. Although the working hours reduced dramatically, because the time from dawn to dusk was so short, the work increased sharply. The base was close to the sea and the bad weather had the effect of pushing large gull populations inland. Every morning we would be greeted by the sight of the runways being practically blanketed in gulls. Lanner and lugger falcons were not going to move large birds like greater and lesser black backed gulls, so now we employed peregrines and saker falcons. But each time we managed to move them off another wave would come in. It was a constant battle to keep the runways clear. In fact we used to pray for foggy days when the base would, to all intents and purposes, shut down. Despite the proximity of the sea, however, these were, unfortunately, few and far between, although at least now we were only on call from 8 am to 4.30 pm. This was much different from the summer when the two-way radio had to be on and attended for sixteen hours a day.

The gulls were a different proposition to other bird species and the peregrines were encouraged to pursue them hard. A peregrine in business mode very soon shifted them, as did one of the saker falcons we flew at the time. She was a very large saker and had come from the hawk market in Damascus. She relished flying gulls and would catch one almost daily, always subduing them very easily: we could take them off her undamaged most of the time. We would then release the gull and it would disappear rapidly, squawk-ing at the indignity of it all. This squawking had an immediate effect on any other gulls in the area and the whole lot would lift up and wheel into the sky and move on.

We did hit one sticky patch on this base, but it did not last long. A new commander was appointed and he was sceptical, to say the least, about the merits of employing a falconry unit. Of course he did not arrive at his flight line office until ten each morning. Before then, long before then, we had ensured that the base was clear of birds. When he looked out of his windows each morning he did not see flocks of birds milling around his air base. He decided, without consulting the control tower, the pilots or others who knew what it had been like before we arrived, to suspend our activities. It was made plain to us that he would leave things to nature for a week and then review the situation. If, at the end of that week, as he suspected, there would be no marked increase in bird life then steps would be taken to end the contract for bird control. We vainly tried to explain what would happen but we were not listened to.

I asked if this suspension meant that we were to remain on call in case of a decision reversal. An emphatic 'No' was the reply. The next morning, therefore, my fellow worker and I took ourselves off hunting for the day. We returned around seven that evening to be greeted with an urgent summons to the base commander's office. We pointed out that our services had been temporarily dispensed with and that we had other plans for the evening. (Of course we hadn't, we were just making a point.) Ten minutes later the base commander himself was knocking at the door. He came straight out and admitted that he was wrong and that he had been hasty. Apparently the base had been teeming with birds all day. Several near-misses had occurred and the pilots wanted the falconry unit back in business as quickly as possible. We got two falcons ready and went out with him there and then, so he was able to watch first hand the effect the falcons had on the flocks. He was impressed, to say the least. After this he became one of the unit's greatest fans and would proclaim the excellence of our work to all that would listen. In fact he became hooked on falconry as a sport and would often join us when we were hunting on land around the base. The one good thing that came out of the whole affair was that he saw our living conditions for himself. By the end of that week we were relocated in much better accommodation.

Once we had got ourselves a decent routine worked out for dealing with the influxes of birds that the weather conditions brought, we could sort out some serious hunting. My colleague and I worked out a system whereby one of us could get off the base by ten each day and go and fly falcons properly. By ten the back of the work had been broken and that meant that one person could cope admirably on his own. The other was then free to spend the rest of the day hunting. The local farmers were very good and gave us permission to hunt rooks and crows on their land. The peregrines we used had been got truly fit by flying them in all weathers on the base. The old maxim that if a wild falcon can fly then so should a trained one was true of our team. We were not in a position to tell a base commander that our falcons wouldn't fly because the weather was rough. Only fog and exceptionally heavy rain stopped our flying activities – and this showed in the fitness and condition of the falcons. They were the epitome of health, with a real bloom on their feathers. A slight reduction in their condition and a few days on a rook lure and they were ready. Both of us enjoyed considerable sport of a very high quality and, because we killed a lot of rooks, the farmers were always pleased to see us and we were inevitably asked to come back again.

For pure falconry, then, the winter was the best time for us, but the base in spring and summer was an extremely pleasant place to be if you had an interest in nature. One of the compensations for having to get up so early was the wildlife you could observe having done so. The short grassy areas meant sky larks used to abound. It was lovely to sit in the car and watch a sky lark ring up, emitting its beautiful song as it did so. We could see them so clearly that we could observe the purple colouring inside their mouths. Whimbrels and curlews used to nest close to the base, too, and we would watch them with binoculars. Deer would come and feed close to the perimeter. Strangely enough the one resident I would have expected was sadly missing. No kestrels. This was not due to our presence, as a local bird watcher told us there had been no kestrels there for several years.

We did have a female kestrel that had been passed on to us by a local policeman who had rescued it from some children. This was quickly trained and put out to tame hack. That is, it was left out to fly all day and then called down to a lure in the evening and, having been fed, put in the mews for the night. As it gradually got stronger on the wing it was left out overnight if the weather was good – having been given a meal by us first, of course. After six or seven weeks of this semi-freedom, the kestrel had obviously started to kill for itself. It would still come in to the lure, but its crop would already be bulging with food. When it had come in for seven consecutive nights with food in its crop we decided it was time it stood on its own two feet and made its own way in life.

We ignored its presence and ceased trying to call it in. The kestrel was obviously looking after itself well enough, as we would see it on a daily basis, but it did not bother trying to beg food from us. The only exception to this was the following winter when it came to us a couple of times if the weather had been particularly harsh. We soon learnt where it would normally roost and nearby was a tree stump. When the weather turned bad we would go and put some food on the stump, giving the call we used to give to call her in. Sometimes she would take the food, other times not.

What did astound us was how quickly the kestrel learned to keep out of the way of the larger falcons we flew for the bird clearance work. When we were flying lanners or luggers she would carry on flying round, but she would do so at a discreet distance. When a peregrine or a saker was being flown, though, she would take herself off and not be seen again till the larger falcon was down and back on the fist. She would then appear from nowhere, heck her annoyance at us a few times, and resume her normal routine.

In fact the only wild raptor that gave us trouble on a regular basis was a female sparrowhawk. She nested in a small wood that was in the middle of a highly restricted area. Should one of the falcons stray towards the wood – it didn't make any difference what species of falcon – then she would be instantly out and trying her hardest to drive it away from her territory. She was absolutely fearless, or should that be foolhardy, in her attacks. On two separate occasions she actually grabbed a falcon and tried to bring it down. Fortunately in both incidents the falcons concerned were lanners and they were not at hunting weight. Had it been a peregrine at hunting weight then it would have been a very different outcome for the sparrow-hawk.

We did sometimes have brief visits from the wild peregrines, who would normally only stop over for a very short while before moving on again. Had a peregrine decided to try and estab-lish a territory around the base then life could have been made very difficult indeed for our falcons. We only ever had two bad experiences as a result of the activities of wild peregrines. The first was on a really cold and rainy day when we were flying a male lanner falcon. He had the habit of circling up to a really terrific height and then, when the lure was thrown out, he would just fold his wings and come back down in one long tremendous stoop. Breathtaking to watch.

As per normal, on this day, the lanneret had gone up to a really good height. In fact he was so high he looked like a swallow. I gave a shout and threw the lure out, marvelling at him as he dropped like a stone back towards us. But when he was two-thirds of the way down, and at maximum velocity, a blur just appeared from nowhere, merged with him for a moment, and then was off in a different direction. The lanner seemed to falter for a moment and then spiralled to earth in a very unnatural manner. When he hit the ground in an untidy heap a peregrine tiercel appeared over him and was hecking in anger. I ran to the lanner to save him from the *coup de grâce* that was obviously about to be administered. He was still alive but in a state. The peregrine had hit him hard and had damaged one wing. I scooped the lanner up and took him straight to a vet.

The good news was that apparently nothing was broken. The lanner was groggy for a day or two and so was kept inside in the warm and given as much food as he wanted for a few days. It didn't take him too long to make a complete physical recovery, but his mental recovery was another story completely. He never flew high again and all the time he skimmed round low he was looking above him to see if there was anything there. When he sat out on his block during the day weathering he would be looking constantly skywards. He would often suddenly give his alarm call and when we looked up nothing would be visible to our eye. But on fetching a pair of binoculars and looking in the direction he was, as often as not we would spot a tiny speck in the distant sky. As the distant speck got closer and passed over it would turn out to be a peregrine falcon. Yet he took no notice of the peregrines he shared the weathering ground with.

The other incident was a lot less dramatic but almost had a far nastier outcome. It was an early summer's evening and eleven falcons were sitting out on the weathering ground. I was cleaning out the falcons' night quarters and my companion was out exercising the dogs. Suddenly I heard several sets of bells jangling away and a lugger falcon giving its distress call. I ran round to the weathering to see a big feather bundle rolling around on the ground. The feather bundle turned out to be my lugger and a peregrine tiercel locked together. The lugger was tied to its block so I grabbed the peregrine and roughly pulled it off my falcon. I threw it up into the air so that it could go and I could examine my lugger to make sure she wasn't hurt. Instead of flying off, however, the peregrine dived straight back on her again. I pulled him off for a second time, but this time I put him in a cardboard box. Having inspected the lugger and made sure she was okay (she was, apart from some talon wounds to her feet and dented pride), I turned my attentions to the peregrine. I was reluctant to let him go in the immediate vicinity in case he did exactly the same thing again, so I waited till my companion returned from exercising the dogs. Then I drove the peregrine to the coast, only a seven-mile journey, and then released him there. Fortunately that was the last we saw of him.

All in all, working on the airfield was good fun and gave me plenty of time to enjoy flying falcons. But everything loses its freshness after a while and I decided to move on to something else. One thing was for certain, though: I would never be able to take a normal nine to five job again.

# CHAPTER SIX

# Working the wine gardens

GLANCING through the Sunday papers, my eye was caught by an article on the damage being done by birds to the annual grape harvest in the Burgenland region of Austria. I thought this could be a lead worth following up with regard to bird control work, so I wrote to the Austrian correspondent of the newspaper the article had appeared in and also to a falconer friend in Austria with whom I had been corresponding for several years.

The journalist was very helpful and wrote back with a full account of all that had been going on in Burgenland for the past three years. Apparently the grapes had been severely ravaged each year by huge flocks of starlings that descended on the crops for a month or so before they were due to be harvested. The growers had tried just about everything to shift the starlings but nothing at all had worked. Radio-controlled aircraft had been tried, as had kites and gas guns. One town in particular was being hit very badly and the council and local businessmen were desperate to find a remedy.

My falconer friend in Austria had followed things up his end and had managed to speak with the head of the wine growers' co-operative for this town. He had told him about the work that had been done on airfields to alleviate bird problems. The growers were interested in anything that might help solve their situation and my friend had set up a meeting between the town council and the two of us. Consequently I flew to Vienna and Karl, the Austrian falconer, and I drove to the beautiful town of Rust for the meeting.

The discussions went very well from our point of view and the council were eager to have an accurate costing put forward. I had arranged to stay in Austria for a week and had gone armed with sufficient calculations and paperwork to be in a position to give such information within a couple of days. Obviously there were some variables in costs between England and Austria – such as the renting of accommodation, the price of hawk food, etc. – but these things were soon sorted out and within three days Karl and I were back with a concrete proposal. This was gone through with a fine tooth comb by the council and they assured us of an answer within one month.

I had a couple more days in Vienna sightseeing and then returned to England. I had only been back just over a week when Karl was in contact saying that the proposal had been accepted, in principle, subject to a favourable demonstration. To take falcons from England to Austria for a one- or two-day demonstration was just not feasible. The legislation had recently changed in Britain and we now had import licensing, so it was completely impracticable for me to take my falcons over for such a short stay. The paperwork involved would take too long anyway. Karl had two falcons at the time and through his services we borrowed two more. Four falcons were not really sufficient for the sort of area we had to cover, but for demonstration purposes they would have to do.

So it was back to Rust, via Vienna, and preparations were made for the display that could lead to greater things for Karl and me. The starling problem only lasted for a limited period and was not actually being experienced at the time of the demonstration, but there were plenty of rooks, crows and sparrows around to test the effectiveness of our bird control methods. The lie of the land around Rust was very good for flying falcons and any falcon that made good height would control a large area. I had a couple of days with Karl to fly the falcons and to get to know them before the demo day. Karl had never done any bird control work so he said that we would fly the falcons as I saw fit. The ones he had borrowed for us were two luggers and both went up relatively well. His own falcons were a lanner and a saker. The lanner flew high but the saker had been used for hunting rooks; it flew well enough, but did not gain any sort of height. I thought of a way of using this to our advantage, though, and final preparations were made for the big day.

The arrangement was that on the day in question Karl and I would present ourselves at the mayor's office and first go over any last minute questions that the town council had. Then it was out into the vineyards for the demonstration and back to the offices afterwards for a yes or no to the proposal. When we got to the mayor's office the entire town council were there. The questions they put forward were all easily answered and were mainly connected to the financial side of things. When the time came to set off and give the demo it became obvious that every single member of the council was going to come with us. This was just not going to be practical – but how do you explain to forty people who are willing to invest their money in your services, and more importantly trust you with their livelihood, they they can't all come at the same time?

Then it occurred to me that there was a large hill on the edge of town, from the top of which you could see all of the town and surrounding vineyards spread out before you. I suggested to Karl that he take the group of spectators up on this hill and give a running commentary of what was going on during the demonstration. After all, not all of the group spoke English and my German was nonexistent. The plan was that I would drive around and look for a flock of birds to move by using a falcon, making sure that wherever I operated was in clear view of the gathering on the hill.

I waited until I saw the cluster of cars parked on the hill and then away I went. It was too early in the year for starlings, but sparrows, rooks and various other species were present in abundance. I found an area that was enjoying the attentions of a considerable number of birds and got one of the lugger falcons to fly. I unhooded her and after a quick look round and a rouse, she took off. She flew round in nice large circles, gradually getting higher all the time. I slowly walked forward into the wind to keep her focused and to bring her over the birds. Long before she had reached her optimum height the birds had fled. But I left her up and continued to walk the vineyard. As we progressed birds in front of us were lifting up and moving off. When the entire vineyard was clear I called the falcon down to the lure. Fortunately it was well trained and came straight in. I gave her some food, re-hooded her and put her on a cadge in the back of the car. On returning to the hill I was greeted with lots of smiling faces. Apparently the demonstration was considered a success.

A couple of councillors asked if it would not be more effective if the falcon were to chase the birds and actually catch one. Carefully it was explained that a falcon in the air poses a great deal more of a threat when the birds underneath it are unsure as to whether it has killed or not, but when they see one make a kill they simply return and carry on feeding. They know full well that having just killed, a falcon will not normally hunt again straightaway.

I said we could also demonstrate this fact easily and quickly. Karl looked across at me and it was obvious from his expression that he was unsure what I had in mind. I scanned the ground in front of us till I spotted some rooks out feeding, then I got the saker falcon ready to fly. Now Karl understood and a broad grin spread across his face. I drove off, leaving Karl to be master of ceremonies again, and made my way down to get into position to fly the rooks. As I was in a car it was possible to get very close to them. I slipped the saker falcon out of the car window at them – very unsporting, but in the circumstances completely necessary. The saker flew into the feeding group and grabbed one. The remainder of the group rung up cawing and cursing the falcon. They circled above her giving vent to their feelings. The milling group attracted every other corvid in the area and very soon a large flock had gathered. The point of the demonstration was not lost on the councillors and the contract for a bird control unit was signed that afternoon.

I returned to England and started to make preparations to move to Austria. The contract was due to start in eight weeks' time and there was a great deal to get done. The prime concern was getting export licences for my falcons. This involved a lot of red tape, particularly when you bear in mind this was in the days before domestically produced raptors. All my falcons had been taken as passage or haggard falcons abroad anyway, but red tape never changes and the falcons could not be moved abroad without individual export licences. This meant endless phone calls, visits to vets, forms to fill in, etc. Then I had to find an airline that would deliver the falcons safely to Vienna airport. It was vital that the falcons got there and through customs as quickly as possible. The last thing anybody wanted was to have them hanging around somewhere.

Eventually everything did get sorted out and the falcons flew to Vienna in style. They each went in individual carry boxes and on arrival in Vienna were cleared through customs within a couple of hours of landing. I had spent a great deal of money getting the falcons over to Austria, which left less than I would have liked for me. I ended up going over on the train and ferry, a horrendous twenty-five hour journey that I would never repeat under any circumstances. But when I did get to Vienna the sun was shining and Karl was there to meet me. We set off on the two-hour journey for my new home town of Rust (pronounced roost) and, despite my excitement, the rigours of the journey meant that I slept all the way. As part of the contract, the town council had provided us with a lovely house on the edge of town. It had a very large and well-shaded garden for the falcons to put out in to weather daily. A big, airy cellar was quickly adapted to make a superb mews for the night time requirements of the falcons.

What did make a lasting impression on me was the warmth of the local people. With the awarding of the contract the local media had gone overboard with their coverage of the situation. I suppose this was because it was so very different from the run of the mill news stories. The result was that just about everyone who lived in the area knew why we were in Rust and what we were there for. They also knew our names and that I was an Englishman who did not, as yet, speak German. This led to an endless stream of visitors who came along to make sure we were settling in okay and to see if they could do anything to help. Invitations to go and visit local people in their homes and have a meal with them were an everyday occurrence. A local school teacher offered to come round one evening a week and teach me sufficient German to be able to get by. This was an offer I jumped at and one I appreciated very much.

The Burgenland area of Austria is extremely beautiful and Rust is a lovely old town full of charm and historic buildings. It is very close to the Hungarian border and is on the edge of the Neusiedel See, a huge salt water lake, some fifteen miles long and several miles wide. One-third of it is in Hungary and the rest is in Austria, but the strange thing is it is only about six feet deep at any point. At the time I went to Austria the Cold War was still very much a reality and the Iron Curtain was still drawn. Patrol boats used to cross back and forth over the See on the Hungarian side to stop people escaping to the west. Two miles or so out of Rust was the Hungarian border and I was taken to see the rows of fencing, minefields and cleared ground that were all in place to keep Hungarians in and others out. A very sombre place.

Situated where it was, Rust was a major tourist attraction and this was to play a big part in our summer there. The contract was an all year round one, despite the fact that the starlings were only a problem for a limited period. The town council wanted the falcons to be there all the time to clear any other birds should they materialise. We had explained that we wanted to be there for a minimum of three months before the starlings were due anyway. This was to enable us to get the falcons fully fit and both them and us familiarised with the area.

Within a week of getting set up in Rust, the whole team of falcons was flying loose and working their way towards fitness. Karl and I would try and fly them in a different location each day so as to get them fully acquainted with the area. The whole scenario was an extremely pleasant one. As we flew the falcons, the locals in that particular area would stop their work and watch them go through their paces. Then they would come over and have a chat, asking questions about what would happen when the starlings came. We would reassure them that the falcons would deal with them and that this season their harvest would be safe.

Once the falcons were really fit and flying well the town council set up a meeting and requested Karl and me to attend. This turned out to be an appeal to help them boost the tourist trade for the area. Close to the See the town had an area of leisure facilities and what they wanted was for us to fly some falcons there each day at a regular time. They could then advertise what was going on and hopefully draw a few more visitors away from their neighbouring rivals. We were more than happy to help as they were paying our wages and the falcons were truly fit now anyway.

These daily flying displays turned out to be a far greater success than anybody could have imagined. Right from the word go they would draw very large crowds. Some of the falcons were not too keen on flying to a lure in front of large numbers of people, so these would be exercised in another area in the morning. But those that would tolerate large numbers of people were flown each afternoon before ever increasing crowds. The town did not charge the public for this daily display and so it certainly did have the desired effect of drawing more and more tourists into Rust. In fact it became so popular that when the work against the starlings started in earnest, we had to get another person in and leave a couple of falcons with them to carry on the displays.

On the bird control front things were, meanwhile, progressing as they should. We had established a routine for flying the falcons that covered every single acre of the ground we were responsible for at least three times a day. We were using mainly lanner and lugger falcons, with the saker falcon that belonged to Karl and three peregrine falcons. The lanners and luggers were encouraged to go up on the soar and given the region we were in, with its terrain and summer heat, this was very easy. The falcons were gradually conditioned to be up for thirty to forty minutes at a time and the heights they achieved meant that they controlled a large area each time they flew. With the team of falcons that we had it meant that each bird flew twice a day and we had sufficient numbers to have a falcon in the air practically all day. The saker was used for hunting rooks and crows, as was one of the peregrine falcons. The other two peregrines were used for bird clearance when a straightforward attack was needed.

A great many falconers, from all over Europe, came to visit us while we were in Rust. They had heard about the project and were keen to see it and to meet the people carrying it out. Some brought hawks or falcons with them and would stay for a while and hunt the local area. We even received a visit from a foreign falconry club official who declared he would make us honorary members of his club. Quite why he should do this I could not think, and in any case he was far too interested in consuming the local product to come out and see the falcons fly. But most who came to visit were pleasant and wished us well in our venture.

Being surrounded by all these beautiful falcons and actually doing very little falconry began to make me frustrated. To overcome this I purchased a red headed merlin from India and a goshawk from an Austrian falconer in Vienna. This falconer had obtained a male and a female and had decided to keep the former and dispose of the latter. I drove to Vienna to collect the goshawk and had arranged to meet him at his centre. When he said centre, I had naturally assumed it was a falconry centre that was open to the public. But this was very far from the case. The small centre was for the use of this falconer and a few of his friends; it was only about an acre square and was surrounded by a wooden fence. There was no lock on the gate and inside all the hawks, falcons and two eagles were sitting in weatherings that had no fronts on them. Apparently the wives of these falconers objected to hawks in the house so the friends had got together and purchased a small field. They had then turned it into a mini-centre, for their own use only. Needless to say there was a shed that had a freezer in it for keeping hawk food and a fridge for keeping the beer in. A few benches and chairs were scattered around and it was their custom to meet in the evenings after work and at the weekends. In this way their falconry did not intrude on their home life. They had some beautiful hawks including a magnificent golden eagle and three hobby falcons.

What struck me more than anything else was that nothing was locked up or seemed to be secured in any way. When I asked about this it was explained that falconers in Austria did not suffer with the thefts that we in England did at the time. Their only concern was stray dogs and foxes, hence the fence around the perimeter which was electrified along the top. There was no lock on the gate because it was not considered necessary. Also, if a local resident wished to show someone the hawks it would be inconvenient if the gate were locked and there was no one there to unlock it. With all the petty and often pointless theft in England, plus mindless vandalism, it was a situation I just could not comprehend.

I duly collected my goshawk, a passage female, and handed over the vast sum of £3 for her. She had already been manned and flown to the fist so it was merely a case of a little retraining and we could start hunting together. By the time I got back to Rust it was very late indeed. Out of sheer laziness I put the goshawk out on a bow, instead of putting her away in the mews properly, and went to bed. The next morning over breakfast I was telling Karl what a nice looking goshawk she was and how pleased I was with her. He asked where she was so he could have a look. I said in the garden on a bow. He said she definitely was not as he had already been in the garden to refill the falcon baths for the day. We both rushed out into the garden and sure enough the sight that greeted us was one exceedingly empty bow perch.

The chances of recovering the goshawk looked pretty grim. We had no idea how long she had been gone or in what direction she had taken off. Worse still, she had gone off because the leash had snapped. It was the old-fashioned leather type and had snapped clean through. This was all my own fault as I had intended to change the leash when I picked the goshawk up to feed it that day. I should have changed the equipment on the goshawk when I got home the previous night and certainly ought to have taken the trouble to put her away in the mews properly. The only thing that might be in our favour was that her previous owner had not fed her on the day of collection in case she was car sick on the way back, and I had not fed her on our arrival back in Rust because of the lateness of the hour. At least she should be hungry.

Now, thanks to my laziness, the poor goshawk had gone off with jesses held together by a swivel and half a leash dangling down. Sooner or later it was bound to get caught up and hang in a tree, where it would suffer a slow and miserable death. I cannot ever remember feeling so low and so thoroughly ashamed.

As we walked round to the front of the house to get into our cars and start what would no doubt prove to be a futile search, the postman arrived. He was his normal happy self, which was extremely irritating in the circumstances. When he asked what was wrong I told him. He said that there was a big hawk sitting on a fence post a few yards back down the road. I grabbed a glove and some food and rushed off in the direction he indicated. Sure enough, there was the goshawk sitting on a post. Not only that, but she had one foot tucked up and looked very content. I approached slowly, offering a large amount of food on the glove. She looked at me and flew straight to the fist without a moment's hesitation. She fed calmly as we walked home and was oblivious to the elation we all felt that she was safely back.

This had not been the sort of start to our career together that I would have hoped for. First job when I got her back home was to fit a complete new set of equipment. Grumpy, as the goshawk became known, was a good hunting hawk and we had many good flights together. The area had plenty of rabbits and quite a few hares. She took rabbits with no problem at all and caught a fair number of hares. Being a passage hawk she had probably encountered them in the wild. She knew the trick of grabbing them by the head and then transferring one foot to the rear loins. This way they were immediately immobilised and she was in instant control.

Most of the hares she took were flown in the vineyards, where the vines were grown on frames in straight lines. I would walk along a headland at the edge of a field and peer down each row. On spotting a hare I would raise my fist gently and the goshawk would be off after it in a flash. The hares would initially evade her by switching rows at the last minute as she closed on them but, having lost a few in this manner, she soon learned to hurl herself over the top of one row and into another. She got very deadly at this and would even fly down the row next to the hare and flip over at the last minute, taking the hare completely by surprise.

The one quarry that eluded her was duck. She would fly these with an absolute passion, yet she never managed to catch one. Most hawks learn very quickly what they can and what they can't catch. But duck was something she would always try for. She would take on astonishing length slips at them, but always failed to close right up on them. Once the ducks realised that she was in pursuit they would pull away rapidly from her. Still she insisted on flying them.

One species she did catch, no matter how much I tried to

discourage her, was hoopoe. These startlingly beautiful birds, with their orange, black and white plumage, drew her like a magnet. Hoopoes appear to be very clumsy in flight, but are in actual fact highly manoeuvrable and quicker than most people give them credit for. Grumpy would follow every twist and turn of their flight, however, and catch them with what looked like considerable ease. Whenever I spotted that she was looking to fly a hoopoe I would hang on to her jesses and hold her back. But sometimes she would be bobbing her head and I would not see what it was that had caught her attention. Assuming that it was a hare or a rabbit I would hold her up. Only when the flight was well and truly joined would I realise what her intended victim was. And by then, of course, it was too late to stop it.

I eventually lost Grumpy in very unfortunate circumstances. We were hunting some arable land on the edge of town. It was an area that always held rabbits but care had to be taken when slipping a hawk there. There were also a large number of grass owls, very similar to our short eared owls, so I would not let Grumpy leave the fist unless I could see the rabbit myself. On this fateful day I had seen two rabbits out feeding and Grumpy tightened all her feathers and leaned forward – a sure sign that she had seen them too. I held up my fist and she was off and closing very rapidly on the rabbits. At the last minute she swerved to one side and crashed headlong into a small bush. Instantly a most terrible noise came from that area but, before I could get there, a pine marten emerged with Grumpy in its mouth. On coming face to face with me the animal dropped Grumpy and made off. The goshawk had been bitten horrifically in the chest and died within a couple of minutes. Her bravery and confidence in her own abilities had been her undoing. I shall always remember her with affection.

The red headed merlin that I purchased from India was a dashing little falcon with which I had many hours of fun. His training was very straightforward and I was hunting him four days after collecting him from Vienna airport. Being so small he was used for hunting sparrows and similar sized quarry, but would on occasion tackle pipits. These always proved to be very good flights, like scaled-down rook hawking. The flights at sparrows were more like flying a long winged sparrowhawk. He would spot his prey and fly directly at it, grabbing it before it put into cover – and as often as not taking it after it had put into what it thought was cover. Bushes and trees would not deter him from getting his prey. I lost Noddy, so called because of his habit of nodding his head so repeatedly before taking off, after five weeks of hawking together. He chased a starling out of sight over the Hungarian border and I never saw or heard of him again. But he was fit and killing well so there was no reason, that I could see, why he would not have survived.

After several months of living an ideal existence the arrival of the starlings came as a very large shock. Right from the outset we had heard that the numbers involved would be mind boggling. First of all we had taken the numbers with a pinch of salt, and second we had wrongly assumed that the starlings' arrival would be a gradual process. We had envisaged that we would start to see one or two small flocks and that, as the days progressed, these would grow in number and content. Just shows how misguided you can be.

Karl and I were on a hill preparing to fly one of the lanner falcons when he pointed into the distance at what appeared to be a black storm cloud. Neither of us could understand how such a cloud could appear in an otherwise clear sky. We carried on with what we were doing and put the lanner falcon on the wing. As she circled up into the sky the storm cloud fragmented momentarily, then bunched back together and drifted away, in the direction it had come from. It was a huge flock of starlings. This scene was to be repeated five more times that afternoon. It was almost impossible to estimate just how many starlings were in those clouds but it was certainly hundreds of thousands.

According to the local World Wildlife Fund representative, the starling numbers that decimated the crops in the area each year were between ten and twelve million. He had serious doubts as to whether our falcons would be able to do more than irritate the starlings briefly. The main body of the invasion force roosted in Hungary and foraged into Austria each day to eat. We took up station on our hill at first light each day and flew eight falcons one after the other. Having reached number eight we would go back to number one and fly them all again. The problem we had was that at first light it was still cold, none of the falcons would make spectacular height until the sun had warmed up the ground. By flying constantly, though, we did manage to keep the hordes at bay. Once we got to mid-morning the starlings had already accepted the situation and had gone to other vineyards to feed. Our area was free of starlings.

It became evident that the hill we used as a base was the main crossing point for the flocks. If we could keep them from crossing over it then our area would escape their attentions. If some did get through, which inevitably did happen from time to time, then one of us would go to lower ground and fly a peregrine falcon near them. This made them leave immediately. After the first week we considered we were doing a pretty good job. Very few starlings were getting through and those that did were moved on. We decided then that we did not have a high enough profile ourselves. We were doing our job, and it was successful, but we were not being seen to be doing it. So once the mid-morning point had passed we would drive around the vineyards, flying a falcon at random just so that the locals could see we were working.

One bird we had to avoid disturbing at all costs was the stork. These nested in large numbers on the rooftops of Rust and were considered good luck omens. So keen were the locals to have them that they would put up elaborate metal structures around their chimneys to encourage the storks. Despite the fact that we had some fifteen or so raptors in our garden a pair of storks chose our house to nest on. Beautiful though they undoubtedly were, they made a great deal of noise and a considerable mess. It was nice to see them fly out each morning in search of food, however.

The local bird that gave me most pleasure was the saker falcon. There were several in the vicinity of Rust and they were more tolerant of human presence than peregrine falcons. I spent many hours watching them hunt and, later in the year, raising their young. A booted eagle was also resident in the area and this would hunt for rodents and snakes in the fields around the See. While watching it hunt one day I saw a wild peregrine falcon come in and give it a hard time. Having seen the eagle off the peregrine perched on the telegraph pole to rest. Through the binoculars I could clearly see the telltale cheek patches of a calidus peregrine, the first one I had ever seen in the wild.

Our success unfortunately proved to be other areas' downfall. The starlings that could not feed with us soon found alternative sites. The normal deterrents of fire crackers, kites and gas cannons just did not work against such sheer numbers. Karl and I soon had representatives from other local councils coming to see us, to try and get us to work for them. We explained we were under contract and there was no way we could, or wanted to move. Rust had been very good to us and we owed them our loyalty.

The period of hectic flying lasted just over five weeks. I have to say that at the end of it both the human and avian elements of the team were very tired indeed. We had been fortunate in that we only lost one falcon during this period of activity and she had gone up on the soar and drifted away never to be seen again. There was no telemetry in those days, not that it would have done any good as she was last seen well inside the Hungarian border. It was out with a lure each morning and give her a while to come in. I think she left the area altogether quite quickly, though, because otherwise the daily flying of the other falcons would surely have brought her in.

Once the grapes had been harvested the whole area relaxed. The falcons were fed up and only four were kept flying just in case they were needed. After a week or so it became apparent that they wouldn't be required so they were stood down as well. It was nice to be able to give the falcons as much as they wanted to eat each day and let them just enjoy themselves weathering and preening.

In October the town held its wine festival and the falconers were the guests of honour. It was a lovely week, when the wine flowed and everyone was happy. I had decided to return to England and try my hand at a business venture I had in mind, so the festival felt like a good note to end on and turned into a bit of a leaving party. I had made a great many friends in Austria and would miss them and the countryside. My falcons and I, almost reluctantly, returned to the cold and damp of England.

CHAPTER SEVEN

# Across the pond

AMERICA was a country that I had never had any real burning desire to visit, unlike so many of my friends. But when the opportunity of a free air ticket came up and it coincided with a falconry meet I made the effort and went. The meet in question was being held by the North American Falconers Association and was at Kearney in Nebraska. The free ticket I had was a return to Denver, Colorado. Looking at a map it didn't seem too much of a drive from Denver to Kearney, perhaps a day at the most. In the end three of us made the journey over. I think one of the reasons for my lack of interest in visiting America previously had been my intense dislike of flying. The thought of a ten-hour flight to Atlanta and then another two-and-a-half hours on to Denver did not fill me with pleasure.

Our arrival in Denver was relatively late and we were all tired from the flight anyway. We decided that the best plan of action was to get a hire car sorted out, then find a motel for the night. This way we could start off suitably refreshed in the morning. The meeting didn't start for another three days so we had plenty of time to make our way slowly across this part of America and take in a few of the sights.

The next morning saw us negotiating our way out of Denver and onto the interstate highway. This proved to be a lot easier than we had imagined. We had no sooner cleared the suburbs of Denver than we saw a large raptor sitting on a telegraph pole. As we got closer we could see it was a male golden eagle. We were staggered.

Imagine leaving somewhere like Manchester and seeing a goldie sitting beside the main road. We stopped and took photographs of it and after a few minutes it took off and flew away in leisurely fashion. Less than a mile down the road was another one – again a male and again totally unconcerned as we took photographs of it. As we got into more open countryside we started to see red tails and ferruginous hawks in ever increasing numbers. With the first dozen or so a cry would go up from the person who'd spotted it and the car would slow and we would all stare at it. After an hour of driving it was merely 'There's another red tail over there.' I gave up counting after forty-five of them.

My first love has always been falcons and I was hoping to see some prairie falcons in the wild. But our first encounter with a wild falcon was with the diminutive little American kestrel. In fact we had to do an emergency stop to avoid hitting it. The kestrel had killed a small rodent beside the road and taken off with it but, due to its lack of size, it was having trouble gaining height and flew right across in front of us. We saw several more sitting on telegraph poles and a dead one on the side of the road. They really are beautiful little falcons with the most vivid colouring.

We stopped for lunch at a roadside diner and as we pulled into the parking bay a prairie falcon took off from the roof of the building. We scrambled out of the car and watched it hunting the fields in front of it. It chased a flock of small birds, failed to catch one, and then flew off. As we sat and had lunch it occurred to us that we had seen more wild raptors in three-and-a half hours than we would expect to see in a month or more back home. The rest of the journey to Kearney was the same. Red tails everywhere. A couple more golden eagles and quite a number of bald eagles. When we spotted the first one we stopped the car in order to photograph it. Having taken several shots I got the camera ready to get it in flight as it flew off. However, it was perfectly happy where it was and completely unconcerned about us. In the end we had to shout and wave our arms to get it to fly and then it only moved to the next tree, a distance of less than thirty yards away.

We saw several more bald eagles in ones and twos but the nicest sight of all was thirteen sitting together in one small tree.

We also spotted quite a few harriers, but were unable to determine which species. They appeared to be marsh harriers, but we never got close enough to be completely sure. We spotted a Cooper's hawk sitting in a tree but as we slowed to get a closer look it was off in a flash.

One thing we did notice as we drove for hour after hour was that every small town we passed by was apparently the home of Wild Bill Hickok. He must have had an extremely restless childhood, moving around as much as he evidently did. What did strike us, and left a lasting impression, was the vast openness. It was what we had expected, but it was still stunning. I like solitude and being able to see for literally miles without much sign of human habitation was like heaven to me.

We eventually reached Kearney and found a motel. The next day we visited Cabella's, probably the largest and most famous hunting store in the world. It was the size of a hypermarket, but devoted purely to hunting. With the exception of falconry equipment, I don't think there was a field sport that wasn't catered for. Some of the items on sale would be frowned upon here and a great many would certainly be illegal. There were stuffed creatures everywhere, ranging from raccoon and beaver to grizzly and polar bears. It was an interesting place to visit but a little extreme for my taste.

The hotel where the main body of falconers were staying was on the edge of town and we went across in the afternoon to see who had arrived. The first thing that struck us as we pulled into the car park was the size of the weathering ground. Or rather grounds, plural. A large area either side of the main car park had been cordoned off and given over to weather the hawks and falcons. What was nice to see was that one side had been allocated to hawks and the other to falcons. Although there were only half a dozen or so trained hawks and falcons out at this particular time, the arrangement was evident by the fact that one lawn had only bow perches on it and the other only blocks. The weathering was also attended and on talking to the man with that unenviable job it would seem that it was manned all the hours of daylight for the entire meet: a very sensible idea and one that falconry clubs over here would do well to follow. Also this attendant really was in charge. What he said was law. He checked the equipment on the hawks and falcons to be weathered to make sure there was no chance of an accident. If he said something had to be changed, it had to be done before the hawk concerned could go out with the others.

On entering the hotel we bumped straight into another group of British falconers, all well known to me. According to them there were several more falconers in the bar – where else? Three of these were also British and known to me, so we had a long chinwag and a few drinks. We also got into conversation with some American falconers and from what they told us it was going to be a very well-attended meet. As time wore on the bar filled up and one or two people even had falcons with them. Later one of these so-called falconers tried flying his falcon in the bar area and made an utter fool of himself. His fellow falconers were also highly displeased with his display and gathered him and his falcon up and removed them from the bar. It would appear that no matter where you go there is always at least one person who is not happy unless they make a spectacle of themselves. The following morning he was conspicuous by his absence. It would have been a great shame if the hotel management had been upset by the incident as they were more than happy for falconers to have their hawks or falcons in the room with them at night, something that not too many hotels would be willing to tolerate.

The next day was registration day and the main body of falconers arrived in a constant trickle all day. On registration everybody received a meet pin and a print produced specially for the occasion. The weathering grounds were filling up rapidly and what a magnificent sight they were. I don't think I have ever seen so many different species of hawks and falcons at any one time. Unlike here, Harris' hawks were in the minority with red tails and goshawks being the most common raptors present. On the falcon weathering there were some magnificent looking falcons, including gyr falcons and gyr hybrids. Without doubt two of the prettiest hybrids were gyr/merlins, known as gyrlins, and peregrine/merlins, known as perlins. There was also a smattering of rather unusual falcons, such as a macropus peregrine originally from Australia, a barbary falcon, a red naped shaheen and two large dark peales peregrines. There were also two pure anatum peregrines. This was the native species of peregrine that was almost totally eradicated by pesticides. These were the first two I had ever seen.

As we stood admiring the perlins one of the owners came over and got into conversation with us. He ended up kindly inviting us to go out and see his and his friend's perlins flying the next day. We readily accepted. I had flown merlins back in England and peregrine falcons for many years. It would be interesting to see what a combination of the two flew like. The two perlins we would watch fly were both female and flew at around eleven ounces, some three to four ounces heavier than a pure merlin. As well as the merlin crosses there were also some pure merlins on the weathering ground. We have the one race of merlin in Britain, but America has three and an example of each was present. One of the races is almost black. These really are beautiful and this was the first one I had ever seen in the flesh.

That evening there was the welcoming ceremony and a couple of state officials gave advice regarding local hunting laws and areas to hunt. The hunting laws differ from state to state and these talks were designed to make sure there was no confusion. Maps were provided that showed where it was possible to hunt without getting landowners' permission. America has vast tracks of land that anybody can hunt on, providing they have a hunting licence. In conversation with some falconers I explained how much we spend to rent a grouse moor in Scotland each year. They were flabbergasted, not at the amount it cost but by the fact that we in Britain actually have to pay. It was something they just could not comprehend.

The week's schedule was outlined and some very interesting talks had been laid on for the evenings. These ranged from breeding and veterinary topics through to new thoughts on training. The organisers had put up two lists in the reception of the hotel. One was for falconers willing to take spectators out and the other was for spectators to put down what they would like to go out with. Room or phone numbers were left on the list so that people could make contact with each other. From what I could see no one appeared to use the lists at all. I think that, like ourselves, people just got into conversation and invitations sprang up naturally as a result.

Bright and early the following morning we were at the hotel reception waiting to meet our hosts for the day. We had a two-hour drive to the ground we were going to hunt and the main quarry was to be the meadow lark, a sort of cross between a yellow wagtail and a sky lark. The area we were hunting was open farmland that had been ploughed over, huge fields sur-rounded on all four sides by ditches. The plan of action was that as we walked across a field the meadow larks, having seen us, would take cover in the ditches. Once they had taken cover one of the perlins was put on the wing. The first one to fly waited on really tightly and at about forty feet. As the meadow lark was flushed the perlin would put in a series of short stoops, trying to grab the lark. The lark made the safety of the ditch again and the perlin waited on right over the spot. As the lark was flushed again the perlin took it on the rise. Six more flights followed and three more larks were taken, all in the same manner.

It really was miniature game hawking without dogs. We were taking the place of the dogs by doing the running around and flushing. It was a very enjoyable afternoon and both little falcons flew extremely well. Not a branch of falconry that I would like to take up myself, it was good sport nevertheless. I would have liked to have seen the two perlins flown together, that is in a cast. With their tight waiting on and their ability to change direction so rapidly it would have been a very pretty sight.

The next day we had arranged to go out with two falconers who flew prairie/peregrine hybrid falcons. Both of these falcons had been flying pheasant and, according to their owners, taking them regularly. Another two-hour drive was called for to get us to the hunting ground, a vast expanse of what had been maizefields. The stalks were laid over on the ground and the landowner assured us it was 'crawling with longtails'. Well, we had picked the one day they weren't crawling. After four-and-a-half hours of walking we had not seen a single pheasant. There were plenty of signs of pheasants and I think that a dog may well have helped the situation. Everyone agreed to call it a day and return to Kearney. Before the return journey, the two falcons were put on the wing, one at a time, and given a pigeon. This was to keep them in a hunting frame of mind and meant that as far as they were concerned the day was not a complete blank.

Then it was the two-hour drive back to the hotel again. This was something we found hard to adapt to. The openness of the country means that distance is of far less significance. People do not think twice about driving a couple of hundred miles to hunt.

Back at the hotel different events had been laid on for each evening, either a speaker or a film show. There was also an area where falconers could put goods out that were for sale, and there was something for everybody – whether it was hoods, bells, videos, falconry art or T-shirts. I spent most of my money here, vowing, each night that I had spent enough and that I would refrain from spending any more the following night. But each night I would buy something else that was 'absolutely essential'.

Day three saw us off with another two falconers, again with hybrid falcons of the prairie/peregrine variety. We went in search of pheasant or duck, and it was only a one-and-a-half hour drive this time. There were ducks in abundance and the first flight was a complete success. The area we were hunting was literally littered with small ponds, nearly every one with some duck on it. It was a case of studying the pond with binoculars and seeing if the situation was right for a flight. We eventually spotted a good set-up and quietly got ourselves into position. The falcon was unhooded and allowed to take off in her own time. She quickly towered up over the small pond. The higher she got the more reluctant the ducks were to take flight. When everything was just right we rushed forward and a small group of mallard rose. The falcon turned over and cut one down with a magnificent stoop. The falconer decided to feed his falcon up there and then as it had performed really well.

Try as we might we just could not get a flight for the other falcon. We did see plenty more ducks but could not get anywhere near them. Pheasants were as scarce as they had been the previous day: we did not see one. What we did see was a wild goshawk catch a pigeon right in front of us. We were walking around a clump of bushes when a pigeon flew right at us. On seeing us it tried to turn and go back the way it had come. Before it could complete the manoeuvre a goshawk came from literally nowhere and grabbed it, a really beautiful hawk in adult plumage. The way it carried on flying, having plucked the pigeon out of the air, strongly suggested it was a female.

A little further on we disturbed a great horned owl. This took off and flew away at a leisurely pace. It did not seem too concerned by our presence. It had been on the ground eating and the remains of its meal showed that yet another pigeon had succumbed to a predator. Great horned owls are really aggressive towards other predators and many a falconer's hawk has been killed by one.

The falconer who could not get a flight for his falcon decided that he would give his bird a pigeon before calling it a day and returning to the hotel. The falcon was cast off and mounted up very well till it was a good height above the falconer. As it drifted in over the top of him a wild falcon appeared, at least as high again directly over his falcon. A pigeon was thrown out and both falcons stooped, the higher falcon overtaking the lower one and grabbing the pigeon. The speed with which it passed the hybrid was awesome. It turned out to be a grey phase gyr falcon, the first wild gyr falcon any of us, including the falconers we were with, had seen in America. The hybrid gave chase for a while, but wisely gave up after a few minutes – the gyr was almost double its size and would have made short work of it had they come together. We were very lucky to have seen a gyr falcon in this area. They are not resident but pass through on passage.

The hybrid falcon came back overhead very high indeed. Despite a lure being thrown out it was not going to come down. Its blood was up and it wanted a kill. The falconer whose falcon had killed the duck gave a pigeon to the hybrid's owner and when it was in the optimum position for the second time, the pigeon was thrown out. The hybrid stooped and missed by a long way. The pigeon made off at a tremendous pace and the falcon, obviously now dispirited, went and sat in a tree instead of giving chase. The lure was offered again and the falcon took no notice. His owner decided to give him a few minutes and then try again. We took a natural break and were discussing what to do if it would not come down to a lure when we spotted the pigeon coming back. It flew around the tree the falcon was sitting in and actually perched on a branch directly above the falcon. This was too much for the falcon, who took off in earnest after the pigeon. But the pigeon again outfoxed the falcon and headed off into the blue yonder. The falcon went back to the tree. The pigeon came back for a second time and this time pushed its luck too far. As it settled on a branch the falcon grabbed it and they both tumbled to earth. One very relieved falconer got his falcon back. I had never ever seen anything like it before – twice the pigeon had escaped and was away completely free, twice it had come back: very strange behaviour. Had the pigeon not come back and sacrificed itself, the result may well have been a lost falcon. It had certainly shown no inclination to coming in to a lure and there were no more pigeons. British falconers do not use pigeons so it is not a situation that would be encountered here.

The following day saw us out with a gyrlin in the morning and a peregrine falcon in the afternoon. The gyrlin was nowhere near as impressive as the perlins had been. It was a full imprint and therefore screamed the whole time, which was not something that was conducive to making me like it, and it did not fly with anything like the style and panache of the perlins. It also seemed to have much deeper wings, in relation to its body size, than the perlins. This gave it power in a straight line chase but seemed to detract from its manoeuvrability. It did not catch anything nor, to be honest, did it look like catching anything. The arguments about hybrids and the ethics of them will rage on as long as people fly them. All in all I am against them. I think that nature really does know best and has given us perfect hawks and falcons for the sport of falconry, providing the falconer picks a suitable hawk or falcon for his countryside and the quarry available. Trying to engineer bigger, faster, better, more aggressive hawks is something that just doesn't seem right to me. There is no super-predator in nature and if there were it would have a short life, because very soon there would be no prey. Those who extol the virtues of hybrids are as often as not connected with the production of them. It is hard to be unbiased and take a balanced view when you are making money out of something.

I am something of a hypocrite on this subject, though, as I have flown several hybrid falcons myself. On the other hand, they have all been given to me and when it comes to spending my own money and purchasing hawks with the long term in view, only pure breds will do for me. I find it a worrying situation when a peregrine hybrid is far easier to purchase than a pure peregrine. This surely cannot be the way to go. What happens with hybrid falcons that become lost and take up residency in the wild? What effect will they have on wild populations? Even worse, it seems to me, is the crossing of hawk species: Harris' and Coopers hawks, red tails and ferruginous hawks. Why? What can anybody hope to gain other than money?

The afternoon's hawking on that day was far more to my liking. We were out with a peregrine falcon and, for the first time in the week, the falcon was assisted by a dog. Pheasant was the quarry and this time we actually saw some. The falcon was put up over a maizefield and when it had made a good height the dog was sent off. It soon had a point and we made every effort to head the point quietly. We did not quite get round into the right position for the perfect flush before the pheasant broke of its own accord, but the falcon had sufficient height to be in complete command of the situation. She hung in the air momentarily and then started to pump downwards. After several pumps of her wings, to give her initial momentum, she folded them to her side and started to drop like a stone. The pheasant was rocketing away at full speed, but the falcon closed the gap and hit the pheasant with a thud that we could all hear clearly. The pheasant just crumpled and dropped to the ground. The peregrine did one circuit over it, just in case it moved again, and then came in and landed on it. It was a perfect flight and a lovely example of what falconry should be. What also pleased me was that the falconer fed his falcon up there and then the dog was given a share of the kill as a reward for the part it had played in the proceedings. Good dogs make good hawks, of that there is no question, but they seldom seem to get the recognition they so richly deserve. I always make a fuss of mine after a flight at grouse, whether successful or not. Without the dogs there would have been no flight. Regardless of the outcome they have done their part by producing the grouse for the falcon.

The following morning saw us out with a group of red tailed hawks. We saw some good flights and several rabbits were taken. Most of the flying we saw was around ditches where rabbits would be flushed out from the undergrowth, the flushing done by beating the cover with sticks and trampling it. However, one red tail was hunted by letting it go up on the soar. Once it was up a good height the party would walk out line abreast across the fields till a rabbit was flushed. The red tail would then fold its wings and come in like an eagle. It would bind to the rabbit and the two of them would roll over and over – very dramatic to watch. The red tail is a very underestimated hawk over here in Britain, but in America they do have the advantage that they can take passage ones from the wild.

We had to leave after lunch so we had said our goodbyes the night before. Addresses were exchanged with various people and invitations to come hawking were being handed out left, right and centre. I had enjoyed the meeting, but as with all such occasions you only get a flavour of the sport. I vowed to come back and get to grips with the real thing. But one thing that had come across was the genuine hospitality and warmth shown to visitors. We had certainly had a good time and several people had put themselves out in an endeavour to show us sport.

The reason for our early departure was that one of our party had to visit a relation. We would be taking a circumspect route back to Denver, which meant an additional four-hundred-mile drive, something none of us relished. We had been extremely good while driving in America and had observed the speed limit without fail, but with a long haul in front of us one of our party drove at the English speed limit whenever it was his turn at the wheel. He was confident that he would not get caught, but that if he did, being a tourist, he would either just get a ticking off or the fine would be minimal. Wrong on both counts. He did get caught and the fine was over £90 – payable there and then.

As we drove across a particularly barren stretch of landscape we spotted a group of men clustered round some vehicles and thought that one of them had a hawk on his fist. We turned the car around as soon as we were able and made our way back to the group. By the time we got there they were almost ready for the off. The group were falconers, with three Harris' hawks and a spaniel, and they had gathered to hunt rabbits. We explained that we were falconers from England who had come over for the NAFA meet. An invitation to join them for an afternoon's sport was immediately extended, which was gratefully accepted. We set off line abreast with the springer dashing about following up any scents it found. The three harris hawks had been flown together on a regular basis so they were all ready to go. When a rabbit did get up all three would be off in hot pursuit. I forget exactly how many rabbits were caught in the afternoon, but it was quite good fun. On our return to the vehicles a suggestion was put forward that we should join these falconers for a meal. There was a roadside diner just down the road a little way. (Actually it was thirty-two miles but the food was good and so was the company.) Again addresses were exchanged and promises made to keep in touch. I have since been back and gone hawking with the same group and two of them have been over here grouse hawking with me.

On the last leg of our journey we did manage to spot a couple more wild prairie falcons. These are a favourite of mine and I was disappointed that we hadn't seen one flown at the meet. I was flying one at home at the time myself, although mine had come from a breeding project in Canada. The general consensus on prairie falcons in Britain was that they were hard to train and not worth the effort involved. I was enjoying mine very much and found it a hard flyer and very aggressive towards quarry. The opportunity to see them flown in their native country was one of the things that had influenced my decision to come to America in the first place.

We completed our journey and visited the relative. Then it was on to the airport for the long flight home, which gave me an opportunity to reflect on the past few days. If anything at all stuck in my mind about this first trip to America it was the openness and kindness of the people. When they say that you must come and stay you get the impression that they really mean it, as opposed to something you say out of politeness and hope that it never gets acted upon. The other openness that struck me was, of course, the country itself. To be able to walk all day and not see a soul, to be able to drive for hours on end and only see minimal traffic was a delight. The sheer scale of the landscape was very impressive. Would I go again? Yes – without a doubt.

# CHAPTER EIGHT

# Emma and Evie

LIKE many other falconers I laboured for years at my sport, believing that a dog was a luxury and not a necessity. As I came to enjoy game hawking more and more a dog was a very basic requirement that I could no longer do without. I had hawked partridges and pheasants for many years by spotting them with binoculars first and then putting a falcon in the air. It was not the best way of going about things, but flights could be obtained on a regular basis and I kidded myself that a dog would not make a great deal of difference to my sport. But with grouse this is absolutely impossible, for no dog means no flight. I enjoyed hawking grouse with others and always ended up tagging onto parties that had dogs.

When the opportunity arose to hawk over a moor on my own for several seasons the dog issue was one that had to be settled properly once and for all. I had seen just about every pointing breed there is run over heather at grouse and for me the choice came down to one of two breeds, either a pointer or a setter. By pointer I mean what some people mistakenly refer to as the English pointer. There is no such breed as an English pointer; the 'English' part has been tacked onto the name because of the proliferation of foreign breeds.

A friend had a superb working pointer bitch that was in pup to an extremely good dog. I put my name down for a puppy but had left it a little late and was number nine on the list. Nine puppies were duly born but the last one out had been pinched in the process and was having trouble with its rear legs. Despite lots of care and attention, and repeated visits to the vet, it was decided that the kindest thing for the puppy was to put it down.

Two weeks later I got a phone call to say that someone on the list in front of me had dropped out and a bitch puppy was available after all, so at nine weeks old Emma came to join the family. She was a beautiful puppy, basically a white dog with a few orange markings around her head and tail. Unfortunately she came complete with a case of ringworm, but a couple of trips to the vet sorted that out.

At the time I was running the bird of prey shows at Windsor Safari Park and Emma would come to work with me every day. She was so small I used to drive to and from work with her zipped up snugly in my jacket. She loved it and found all the smells and sights of the safari park fascinating. The advantage for me was that she was with me and around hawks and falcons all day long, although I had to pay particular attention to where she was all the time. Among others, a lappet faced vulture known as Albert used to cast Emma longing glances. Even the bald eagle used to look highly interested as the tiny puppy wandered past her. But Emma kept out of their way and managed to grow normally.

Very soon she was old enough to go on little excursions on her own and would wander off at will. She would instantly come back to the whistle so I was not overly concerned when she took her little constitutionals. The nature of the park meant that although she could get close to some highly dangerous animals, such as lions and tigers, she couldn't actually get in with them or them out to her. The places that she found most appealing, and would visit on a regular basis, were the various food outlets at the park. Each morning she would set off and do a round trip, encompassing all the different burger bars and snack food sites.

As she grew I started to include her in the shows by getting her to come out and lie down beside a falcon after it had been flown and called in to the lure. This was easily done by putting a handful of small chocolate sweets next to the lure the falcon was feeding on. The public at the flying displays used to love to see a dog and falcon side by side. For a falconer it is an everyday sight, but members of the general public think that each is in danger from the other and love the fact that the two of them would be happy in each other's company. From my point of view it meant that Emma had something to do each day and it was good training for later life when she would be used for hunting with falcons.

One of the items in the bird of prey show we were using at the time was flying six young barn owls together. Someone from the public relations side of the park saw Emma and a falcon together one day and decided that there would be some usable publicity in this. A photo shoot was duly set up and Emma spent a morning being photographed with barn owls landing on her back. In the end we did manage to get a photograph with Emma lying down and all six of the barn owls perched in a line along her back. It was a lovely photograph, but for some inexplicable reason was never used.

Emma's serious training started when she was six months old. I managed to get up onto a moor for a couple of weeks and spent a lot of time out with her, encouraging her to work. With the first few covies of grouse that she came across it was as if she had literally just run into them by mistake. She showed no signs of having been aware of their presence and totally ignored them when they took off. I found this very strange and very disappointing. Back at home she had, like most pointer puppies, been pointing anything and everything: butterflies, cars, dustbins, drink cans, etc. I didn't know if this was because she was just too young, or if she was a duff pointer that was not going to point game. I came back from my two weeks very downhearted indeed.

I had only been back three days when a friend asked me if I would like to give Emma a run over a moor he had access to in Wales. He mentioned that grouse were exceedingly thin on the ground but it might do the dog some good. I jumped at the chance, although I'd already convinced myself that Emma was going to end up as a pet as opposed to a working dog. We made the long drive to North Wales and, having parked the car, I let Emma have a run around as my friend and I changed our shoes and put on our boots and coats. When we turned around ready for the off there was Emma, on hard point, some thirty yards from us. We were still very much on the edge of the moor and we both assumed that she was pointing a rabbit. We made our way over to her, all the time telling her to stay and that she was a good dog. I managed to get right alongside her and then eased her forward and up shot five grouse. I was like a dog with two tails. My pointer, that I had more or less written off in my own mind to the status of pet, really was a pointer. Twice more that day Emma found grouse and pointed them staunchly. She also made no move to chase them when my walking forward put the grouse to flight, so she had the makings of being a very good dog for grouse hawking.

Just as Emma was coming up to ten months old I was given the opportunity to spend a few days hawking with Stephen Frank in Scotland. As well as being one of the most respected falconers in the world, Stephen breeds first class working pointers and Emma was produced from his kennel's blood lines. Emma made the journey to Scotland with me and we had four glorious days at the tail end of the season grouse hawking. I would take Emma out and run her in the mornings and then go out in the afternoon with Stephen and his pointers. Emma made excellent progress and really started to work very well indeed. At the age of ten months and one day she had her first grouse killed over her by a peregrine falcon.

While staying with Stephen, Emma would be put in a kennel run for the afternoon when we were out hawking. There was no run that was completely empty and so Emma had to share with a nice looking pointer dog. I commented on what a good looking dog it was and was told that it was slow in developing and exceedingly headstrong, but everyone felt that in the long run it would make a very good hawking dog. Life is full of little coincidences and four-and-a-half years later this good looking dog was the father of my next pointer.

Coming back from Scotland I was filled with hope for the next grouse hawking season and could not wait for the months to roll round so that I could hawk properly with Emma. After what seemed like an eternity Emma, myself and three falcons headed north yet again. I had access to a moor in Caithness for eight weeks and had arranged for various friends to come up and stay during that period. From day one Emma was simply superb and worked extremely well. She not only provided flights for me but also for the various guests who came up. In fact, in just that eight-week period seven falconers who had never managed to kill a grouse with a falcon before killed one over Emma. One of the falconers had been going to Scotland for seven years, trying to catch one without success. In less than a quarter of an hour on the moor with Emma and me he had achieved his ambition.

The hardest job I had with Emma during this period was actually to stop her working. Whenever the human element of the party sat down for a rest Emma would be called in and told to lie down. As soon as we took our eyes off her she would be up and running again. Her feet were getting cut quite badly by the burnt heather stalks, but nothing would slacken her enthusiasm for the job at hand.

One lesson I did learn over and over again that season was to trust your dog. Often Emma would come on point and I would think that there couldn't possibly be grouse there, either because we had just flushed some nearby, or the terrain was not conducive to holding grouse. But time and time again she showed my judgement to be lacking. If she came on solid point then there would be grouse there. I lost a lot of flights because of my lack of faith in her and because I hadn't yet learned to read her actions fully.

I also changed my opinion about social hawking during this period. Like many other falconers I had people come up and stay, to come out hawking. Sometimes they would bring their own falcons, sometimes they would fly mine. This was fine. But a couple came up with their own dogs and insisted on running them with Emma. I remember one particular German pointer that would just follow round after Emma. As soon as she came on point this dog would run across and steal her point. Not only that, but he would creep steadily forward every time until he put the grouse up. We did not once get a flight with this dog and what concerned me more was that it was making my dog nervous on the point. Despite tactful approaches the guest still insisted on running *his animal*. In the end there was nothing for it but to ask him to leave. No one was getting any sport because his dog was not working properly.

I also had someone come up for a week who wanted to run his dog for his flights and fly over his dog only. In theory this was fine. It meant that each dog would not have to work too hard and would get a nice rest while the other one was running. But the theory did not work out in reality. The dog brought by the guest would not point grouse, although it would find them unerringly. The minute it got scent of grouse in its nostrils it was off in hot pursuit until it chased them up into the air. The dog's owner kept insisting that it would only do this once or twice and then it would settle down. I never saw it point grouse once in an entire week of working on a good moor that held plenty of covies. I was getting frustrated at the lack of flights and Emma was getting frustrated about the lack of work she was doing. This was the final straw for me. I decided from then on that I would either hawk alone or any guests who came on the moor with me would have to fly over my dog.

Emma also managed to teach me a little about human nature during our first full season grouse hawking. As I said, several people killed grouse for the first time over her. It was interesting to note that those whom I considered true sportsmen would make a fuss of the dog after a flight, be it successful or not. Those who tended to fly hawks more for their ego ignored the dog totally once it had flushed grouse for them. The only reward that a dog asks is that you are pleased with it for the work it has done for you. It does not take a moment to say 'Good dog' and give it a stroke. People who find doing this simple task too much of an effort do not get asked again.

Emma and I happily hawked together for the next couple of seasons and a great deal of it was either on our own or with guests who did not have dogs. As I spent longer and longer in Scotland each year I decided it really was time to get another pointer to ease Emma's work load. I had resisted the temptation previously because home life could get to be a little stretched with two dogs, but happily my wife decided a second pointer was the perfect birthday present and in due course Evie joined our team. My wife had written to Stephen Frank and he had sorted a puppy out for her. All arrangements had been made without my knowing and a gamekeeper who was visiting relatives in the south was going to bring the puppy as far as Stafford. The first I knew about it was that one Saturday morning I was told I would have to go to Stafford that evening to collect my new puppy. Evie had travelled down with three working Jack Russells and a border terrier. Due to various calls the keeper had had to make, the journey took two-and-a-half days. I don't know if this had an effect, but I had horrendous problems with Evie when I first acquired her.

For a start, she was dreadfully timid and the slightest thing would make her go to the toilet. She had an awful fear of vehicles and would not get in one. If I lifted her in then she would burrow under the seat and I would have a devil of a job to get her back out again. Fortunately Emma was a great help. I overcame the problem by leaving the car in my driveway with the doors and the tailgate open and putting water and food bowls in the back. Emma would jump in and out of the car and the puppy would follow. Gradually she got bolder and would get in and out on her own, but it took an awfully long time before she was confident about vehicles in general.

Evie also arrived with a stomach disorder and I very nearly lost her during her first week with me. But my local vet, who is superb with hawks and dogs, sorted the problem out. I do not believe in punishing dogs by hitting them and chastise mine by raising my voice to them. Evie was so nervous, though, that even a raised voice on the television would make her wee with fright. It was a case of treading on eggshells for a long, long time to fully gain her confidence and get her to be truly relaxed. But we did make progress and Evie was introduced to the hawks and falcons as soon as possible. These she took totally in her stride and in fact was almost a little too casual with a large female goshawk. The resulting nip taught her to show hawks a little respect.

I took both pointers out at every opportunity I had and Evie was very soon completely *au fait* with basic obedience. Emma was a great help again, because the puppy would tend to do what Emma did. Evie started pointing a lot earlier than Emma had done. Butterflies, wasps, bees, flowers, even trees would get the classic pointer stance practised on them. She was eight months old when she first went to Scotland and, just like Emma, showed no inclination at all to point grouse in the early days. I made the mistake of keeping Evie on the lead and running Emma for my sport. When the day's serious hawking was over I would then let Evie off and make the long walk home with her running around. I think because she had been on the lead all day watching Emma work, Evie would just go berserk in these sessions. She did not work the ground but tried instead to cover as much of it as possible at full speed.

After a week or so of this, when it was painfully obvious we were not making progress, I tried a different tack. I took her out in the mornings on her own and tried to get her to work. Again she just tore around the moor with no sense of purpose. If she did come across grouse she just ran straight through them. Three days of this had me at the point of wanting to pull my hair out in frustration. Another change of plan was called for.

At this time I had my very good friend Trevor Hill up hawking with me. I told him that the next day I was going to try running Emma and Evie together, to see what would happen. I warned him that the consequences might be a total disaster as far as hawking was concerned, but I was desperate to try and get Evie working. Trevor said give it a go, so the following day we did. The first five minutes were nothing short of chaotic. Emma ran off and started to quarter the ground, Evie chased after her like a lunatic, barking the whole time. I decided to sit on a rock and have a smoke for a few minutes, otherwise I might well have lost my temper with Evie, which would have solved nothing. After a few minutes the barking stopped. Evie was still running around but at a lesser rate and with her nose down.

During the course of the day Emma had four points on grouse and to our amazement Evie backed them each time. I don't think she was actually pointing grouse, she was just pointing Emma because Emma was pointing. Even so, it had to be classed as some sort of progress that Evie held her point until Emma was sent in to flush. I walked home with a far rosier outlook on the future than I had the day before.

All the falcons had flown, with the exception of a tiercel peregrine that Trevor had with him. I left the dogs to run on the off-chance that we might manage to get a last minute flight for Trevor's falcon. When we were within sight of the cars Trevor called out that Evie was on point. When I looked round I could see that was the case and that Emma was backing Evie. I said to Trevor that this would be Evie's first ever point and it was entirely up to him whether or not he flew it. Trevor said he was sure it was a good point and put his falcon on the wing. At the right moment he sent Evie forward and, sure enough, a brace of grouse rose in front of her. Trevor's tiercel cut one down clean as a whistle. All of us were ecstatic. This was Trevor's first ever grouse caught over Evie's first ever point. She was nine months old to the day at the time. I think they must have heard the shouts of joy back across the border in England.

We went out for a meal that night to celebrate and drank quite considerably to the health of both dog and falcon. Over the next six weeks Evie went from strength to strength and showed the makings of a first class hawking dog. Subsequently that season she had forty-odd brace killed over her, as well as a few pheasants.

Evie's one weakness is the blue hare. Given even half a chance she will be off coursing them. The minute I spot one I have to blow the recall whistle and get Evie back in to me quite quickly. She has a real thing about them and just wants to be after them. Brown hares she ignores, it is just the blue that seem to fill her with the wrong kind of desire.

Evie and Emma work very well together and run as two entirely separate dogs. I was worried in the early days that Evie would just run round wherever Emma went, but as Evie's confidence grew she became very much her own dog. On several occasions I have been faced with the situation where both dogs have come on point at the same time, but several hundred yards apart. With a good high mounting falcon this gives the opportunity for a second flight should the first one not end well. The first time the landowner of the moor I currently hawk came out with us to see the falcons fly, just such a situation occurred. I was on top of a hillock, explaining what the dogs were doing, when they both froze on point within a few seconds of each other. They were some three hundred or so yards apart. I put a falcon on the wing and flew over the nearest dog, which happened to be Emma. The flush and stoop were both good but the falcon just failed to make contact. Fortunately it rung back up again to a good height and I walked across to where Evie was still on point. When everything was right I sent Evie in and a nice stoop and clean kill were the result. As it turned out, from a working dog and falconry point of view, the demonstration could not have gone better.

My pointers have provided me with literally hundreds of hours of pleasure on the moors, but also at home as companions. When people drop round to visit they are generally amazed to see that both dogs live in the house. In fact, friends who have hawked with me find it hard to believe that the two couch potatoes draped over the furniture are the same all-action working dogs they have hawked with. Both Emma and Evie have done little bits of television work, in connection with hawking, and have also been used as models for sporting book illustrations.

One of the strangest things we were ever approached to do was find nesting woodcock. A wildlife photographer had permission to film nests in the New Forest, but he was having trouble locating them. I was asked if I would go down and run the pointers for this purpose. We had a lovely day out and a superb lunch, all courtesy of the company wanting the pictures. We found pheasants, deer, partridge and just about everything else – except woodcock.

The last bit of television work we did nearly ended in disaster. I had been asked to provide pointers for a hawk to hunt hedgerows over and to find pheasant for a falcon to fly at. I said that a friend and I could bring the pointers and a hawk and falcon that were used to working with them. The television company informed us they had their own falconer with a hawk but we could bring a falcon. We decided to take a Harris' hawk with us anyway, just in case it was required. I am always dubious about hawks being flown over my dogs, particularly Harris' hawks. On our arrival I was intro-duced to the falconer with the Harris' hawk and expressed my concern to him. He assured me that his Harris' hawk never ever went for dogs and that everything would be okay. Twice more I asked the question, and twice more I was assured I was worrying for nothing.

The idea was to throw the hawk up into a tree and then have the pointer work the hedgerow beneath it. Any resulting flight would then be filmed. I had purchased a new pair of moleskins for the occasion, as my old ones were a bit too battle-scarred for television. The hawk was cast off and at the fourth time of asking went into the tree. It seemed overkeen to me and again I asked its owner if he was sure it was all right with dogs. The reply I got was an extremely curt 'Yes'. Emma was slipped and started to work the hedgerow. The Harris' hawk immediately launched itself out of the tree and attached itself to Emma's face. The owner just stood there saying, 'What do I do?' Telling him in no uncertain terms what he could do, I raced over to Emma (which involved leaping over a barbed wire fence and into a ditch) to pull the hawk off her. I literally threw the hawk away and it swung straight round and latched onto Emma again. I pulled it off again and handed it to its owner, who by this time had managed to get himself there.

Fortunately Emma was not badly hurt: the blood flowing from her mouth was making things look far worse than they really were. I had torn my new moleskins leaping the fence and had managed to submerge one leg in filthy ditch water – not really the best start I have ever had to a day's filming. Very wisely the falconer with the Harris' hawk decided to beat a hasty retreat. The friend who had come along with me to lend a hand if required went and fetched his Harris' hawk, and filming began again. This section was finished without any more trauma.

Next up was supposedly a flight at pheasant with a falcon. We had brought a jerkin with us that waited on really well and flew pheasants with gusto. The land we were on was supposed to be alive with pheasants; after an hour of running the pointers we finally managed to find one. We explained to the film crew how we thought the flight would go and the best position to be in to see all that was going to happen. The jerkin was put on the wing and when overhead the dogs were sent in. A tremendous stoop followed but although he took some feathers out, the falcon failed to stop the pheasant. It then tail chased it for a long way and, having failed, then chased some nearby rooks to vent its anger. After some fourteen minutes of flying the jerkin was brought down to the lure and taken back up on the fist. We asked the television crew what they thought. 'Excellent!' was the unanimous verdict. The next time they would film it. Apparently they had decided to just watch and then film the next flight when they knew what to expect. Needless to say, we did not get another point that day.

As I get older the dog work in falconry has become as important to me as the flight of the falcon. After all, once a falcon has been trained what does it really matter who carries it and releases it? The skill is in the initial training and in picking appropriate flights. In fact you can tell a good falconer more by the flights he refuses than by those he accepts. I find that working the pointers and reading the information they give you is fascinating. Also they are very pleasant companions and such biddable dogs.

I can illustrate very easily the difference a good pointer will make when out hunting, be it with gun or falcon. A few years ago a party of us were invited by the artist Colin Woolf for a day on his grouse moor in North Wales. We met at a prearranged spot and after the introductions were made we set off to make a start. I slipped Emma and told her to get on. I was told that I might as well put her back on the lead as the tract of ground we were crossing did not hold grouse. I was extremely surprised, as it looked ideal. No, I was reliably informed, this piece of ground had been worked by labradors for the past six seasons and there had never been a sighting of a grouse on it. After the fourth point on grouse on this tract of moor it was decided that perhaps walked up shooting over labradors was not the most productive method, and maybe a pointer should be purchased instead.

I do receive quite a few invitations to run my pointers for shooting people, but generally speaking I always decline. Unless I know the gun personally and have seen them shoot I feel the risk to my dogs is far too great. I have shot over them myself a few times, initially just to see what their reaction would be. I would have thought that it would have terrified Evie, but quite the reverse. She loves it, particularly when the grouse drop in front of her. Emma is very laid back about the whole thing and has no interest in them once grouse have been flushed. Yet if we are hawking she watches the grouse after they have been flushed and if the falcon catches one she will run over to it and lie beside the falcon. This trait has proved to be extremely useful on several occasions. If a falcon has killed in long heather, you know it will be close by but you often can't quite locate it exactly. Normally this would mean getting the telemetry out and homing in on the signal. There's no need if Emma is around, though. She will lead you straight to the falcon.

As well as the joy they can give, dogs can also bring tears and tremendous vets' bills. Emma was kicked in the stomach by a cow when she was coming up to three years old. I had to take her to a different vet than normal as I was away from home. The wound was cleaned, Emma was given antibiotics and I was given an extremely large bill. Unfortunately the wound had not been cleaned out properly and Emma had to have a life-saving operation some ten days later. When I got to my usual vet he declared that if I had not brought her in when I had, she would have been dead the next day. Due to this operation Emma cannot have puppies of her own, which is a great shame. I would love to have had one of her puppies to hawk over. But what is not to be is not to be. Emma has served me very faithfully over the years and she has never ever let me down. I shall retire her soon and let her have a few years of working only when she feels like it.

I once lost Evie when a sudden snowstorm literally descended out of nowhere and caught a party of us out on the hill. I think the sudden white-out terrified her and she ran off because of it. After a frantic search of almost two hours I found her at the bottom of a rock face, which fortunately was not too high. She was covered in lumps, bumps and small scratches, but otherwise okay. She was literally curled up in a tight ball and was too frightened to move. Even when I got to within a few feet of her she would not move: I had to slip her lead on and gently encourage her to come home with me.

Soon it will be time to bring another puppy on and I hope that Evie will be as good an instructor as Emma was. But again the puppy will have to be bought in as Evie had a bad case of milk fever during a phantom pregnancy and the resulting treatment meant that she is also incapable of having puppies.

I would not now be without my pointers for anything. Just walking the moors, when I am not hawking, the dogs show you things you would never have seen without them. I remember a later summer's evening a couple of years back when I went for a stroll onto the edge of the moor, just to clear my head. The dogs were running around some way off when they both suddenly stopped dead and came on point. It was obvious from their mannerisms that something was not quite right. In fact Evie actually gradually lay down as if she was setting. Emma was on point but she kept moving her head which was unusual. When I went over to investigate I found they were both pointing roe deer, something they do not normally come across. Evie was pointing the buck and as it got up and took to its heels so did she – in the opposite direction.

No matter how often I am lucky enough to witness it, there is nothing to compare with a pointer running full tilt across the moor and then suddenly stopping dead and freezing in that classic pose they adopt. There is a quotation that is repeated in just about every falconry book: 'Good dogs make good hawks.' There really is no truer saying in falconry than this. But pointers also make good companions and loyal friends.

# CHAPTER NINE

# Hawking days

IN mid-February every year I take advantage of an opportunity to spend two or three weeks hawking on a superb sporting estate near Grantown on Spey in the beautiful Moray region of Scotland. The area is excellent for hawking and watching wildlife and is well known to me and my falconry friends. The keeper on the estate, Drew Young, has been a firm friend for many years and he has taught me a great deal, both in terms of nature and sport. Time spent in his company is always rewarding and enjoyable. I love hawking in Scotland and do so at every available opportunity. The one drawback is the drive up there from home in the south of England.

As normal, this year, I drove up through the night so as to get as traffic-free a run as possible. Even so, it is still a ten-and-a-half hour journey. Hawks, dogs and falconers arrive needing the first day to recover from the journey itself and the day of running around prior to setting off. It is amazing just how much has to be done so that a couple of weeks away will be comfortable for all concerned. Of course things also have to be left so that my business can run smoothly while I'm away.

The human side of things is easy: as much warm clothing as will go in a suitcase and that is that. But for the hawks and dogs a little more thought and consideration are needed. When the vehicle is eventually packed ready to go it is surprising how little room is taken up with human effects as opposed to those of hawks and dogs.

This year a fellow falconer travelled up with me, and as well as my two pointers and falcon we had his personal effects and a female Harris' hawk, but somehow we managed to shoehorn everything in and duly made the tedious drive north. Driving through the night means you miss the vast majority of the traffic, but you also miss seeing the glorious countryside you are travelling through. One or two falconer friends enquired why I was taking a falcon to Scotland in February. After all, game is not in season. Rooks and crows most certainly are, however, and can produce very good flights at this time of year.

The weather forecast for the night we were travelling was for heavy snow in the early hours of the morning. The last time this warning was given and I ignored it I had to wait four hours for a snow plough to clear the road, so this year we set off earlier than normal in the hopes of not getting stuck again. The bad weather failed to materialise and we duly arrived at the keeper's cottage at four o'clock in the morning. We had arranged with him to collect the key to our rented cottage at eight o'clock and have some breakfast with him, so there was nothing else we could do for the next few hours but to try and snatch some sleep in the front of the van. My friend, who is aptly nicknamed 'Drop Off', did precisely that and was dead to the world in minutes.

I could not get to sleep, or even remotely comfortable, and after about an hour of trying, gave up. Instead I quietly got the dogs out of the vehicle and went for a long walk in the pitch dark. It helped pass away a couple of hours. Fortunately the keeper emerged at seven o'clock and we duly went inside for a hot brew and lashings of bacon sandwiches.

Feeling suitably refreshed, we set off to get ourselves unpacked and settled into our home for the next two weeks. As is normal, I am sure, with any falconers, we saw to the needs of the dogs and the hawks first. The hawk and falcon were put out to weather with fresh baths and the dogs were fed, watered and kennelled. Then we got ourselves sorted out and lit the fire in the sitting room to get the cottage warmed and aired. Two more falconers were due to join us and they arrived shortly before lunch, while two red tails and a female goshawk joined the weathering and a springer spaniel joined the kennels. Probably more as a result of ever increasing age than anything else, it was unanimously agreed that a couple of hours' sleep for the human members of the party was in order.

By mid-afternoon everybody had resurfaced and was eager to get out with the hawks. The goshawk and the falcon were both still in training so they were taken to an adjacent field and called off on the creance. The falcon, which had been making splendid progress at home, seemed fazed by the wide open spaces and took an age to come to a dropped lure. The goshawk seemed to be suffering a similar fate and would not come to the fist at all, although it is fair to say that she didn't try and go anywhere else either. Accordingly they were both put away in the mews, having received meagre rations.

The red tails and the Harris' hawk were readied and we set off in search of some rabbits. Due to the journey, none of us wanted to walk too far, so we set off across some fields next to the cottage that normally hold a few rabbits and the odd hare. The red tails, one male and one female, were used to each other and had flown together on several occasions, but the Harris was new to the group. I therefore decided to fly the hawks individually and the two hawks whose turn it was not to fly would be clipped to glove to avoid any accidents. The slipping order was sorted out and it was to be Harris' hawk, then male red tail, followed by female red tail.

The falconer with the Harris walked slightly ahead of the group and was soon off in pursuit of a rabbit that had been flushed by the springer. The Harris chased hard, but the rabbit made cover just in time. At least she had chased instantly and returned promptly to the fist, so she was obviously not suffering any ill effects from the journey.

Next up was the male red tail and he killed within eight feet of being slipped, although it has to be said that a vole is probably not the most sporting or taxing of flights for a falconer's bird. (We only knew that it was a vole because we managed to get a glimpse of its rear end disappearing down the red tail's throat.) But the hawk's owner was pleased because the bird was showing interest, and again was displaying no ill effects from the long drive.

The next flight was a bit more like the real thing. The female red tail was on the right of the party, watching the efforts of the springer spaniel, when a hare broke to the left. The red tail was off after it in a flash. The hare worked its way through some small bushes and the red tail weaved its way in and out of the bushes after it. She really was determined. Despite getting a foot to the hare she failed to hold it, but it was an excellent effort and deserved rewarding.

The falconer decided to feed her up there and then and have her ready for early the following day. The Harris flew another rabbit that was flushed by the springer and took it well, so this hawk was also fed up ready for the morrow. The male red tail was put up in a tree while the scrub around it was worked by the dog. It was hoped that the height would give him an advantage and an early view of any quarry. It did and a mouse was added to his tally. Fortunately for the small rodent population of the area, the weather turned bad on us and we decided to call it a day.

Day two dawned with very overcast skies and the weather threatened to turn very rough. We decided to make an early start and get as much hawking as possible in before the weather intervened. The hawks were out weathering by 7.30 am and preparations were made for a prompt start at 8.30 am. The goshawk and falcon would be left out on the weathering as we intended to do our hawking on a piece of ground that was several miles away. The red tails and Harris were loaded up, along with the springer spaniel. While final preparations were being made it started to snow very lightly. It was more a case of little flurries than constant snow so we duly pressed on with the day as planned.

We went to a farm that had plenty of reed beds and bracken patches and was always good for a few rabbits. The spaniel was eager for the off and was soon working the reed beds with the sort of exuberance that only they can show. He managed to flush a rabbit and the female Harris took off after it. The rabbit was in and out of the reeds with the hawk chasing it hard, but it managed to make the safety of a hole with the Harris literally just inches behind it. The snow was getting a little heavier and the two red tails were taken back to the van to keep them dry.

The spaniel kept working away and soon found a hare for us,

which loped off with the Harris giving chase. The hare ran up and over a small hillock and the Harris put in a dash in an effort to grab it. The animal jinked and set off again, and the harris persisted with its pursuit. She made contact with it but got kicked off. As we approached, the hawk was sitting on the ground and the hare was sitting less than fifteen feet from her. The hare made off at our arrival and the hawk made no effort to give chase. She had obviously received a bit of a drubbing and needed to get her breath back.

The snow was worsening so we decided to go back to the cottage and attend to the hawk and falcon left out on the weathering. On the way back to the vehicle a rabbit was flushed and the Harris caught it after a good chase. When she bound to it she had both feet on the head, but once she had stopped her quarry she transferred one foot to its rear quarters. Thus the rabbit was held fast and was unable to do the hawk any damage with flailing legs. Obviously the hawk had now fully recovered after her hare experience.

When we got back to the cottage we found that the shelter afforded by it had kept the falcon and goshawk perfectly dry. I flew the falcon on the creance and it was a little more receptive, coming twice, quite quickly, although over no real distance. The goshawk was put in the mews as its owner wanted to spend some time with it later on. We had some lunch and then set off with the red tails, neither of whom had flown in the morning. To help ease the springer's work load we took the two pointers with us.

Within five minutes the pointers had found a rabbit, but unfortunately it was very close to a deer fence. The falconer with the female red tail got between the pointers and the fence and the dogs were sent in to flush. The red tail chased initially, then pulled out and went up into a tree. I don't think it was used to pointers and felt a little intimidated by them. The pointers had not chased the rabbit and put the hawk off that way, but their initial surge forward to actually flush is something a lot of hawks that have not worked with pointers don't like. Unfortunately this was the only flight of the afternoon as the snow came on with a vengeance.

It did ease a little towards the later part of the afternoon and the falconer with the male red tail made one last desperate attempt to get a flight for his hawk. The hawk did not think a great deal of the conditions, however, and despite being offered a good slip at a rabbit, took stance in a very tall tree. Once safely perched in the top of the tree it ignored all pleas, endearments and threats regarding coming back to the fist. We all had visions of being out at dawn to try and recover the little angel, but just as the light was fading it grudgingly came down to the fist.

It had not been the most successful day in the history of falconry, but perhaps the weather would be a little kinder tomorrow. As the wind had been so biting everyone thought it best to make sure their hawks had good crops and the dogs were given a thorough rub down and extra food.

A lot of falconers don't seem to realise how quickly hawks and falcons that are already down to their hunting weight can drop in condition due to wind chill. For the smaller species, such as sparrowhawks and merlins, it can prove fatal all too quickly. Even larger hawks such as red tails and goshawks can drop in condition at an alarming rate. Once a hawk or falcon drops below a certain point it is a very difficult job to get the weight to go back on. A lot of people make the mistake of cramming their hawk full of food at one go. This is the last thing you should do. It should be a little and often, and the food should be of high quality and without casting.

The sort of winds we had been out in that afternoon were just the sort to do harm to a hawk, but because we were all aware of it, and the consequences it could bring, we all made allowances for it. I remember a friend with a peregrine tiercel, a few years back, staying out too long in a biting wind. The tiercel had had one tiring flight and the combination of that and the wind chill certainly made him look the worse for wear by the end of the afternoon. It took a great deal of care and attention over the next ten days to get him back to his original flying weight.

The only good thing about bad weather is that it gives the human element of the hawking party an excuse to sit round a blazing fire enjoying a few drams of Scotland's finest.

On waking the next day we discovered that during the night

four inches of snow had been deposited on us and the surrounding countryside. At least the sun was shining, and it wasn't anywhere near as cold as we expected it to be, but the forecast was for more snow flurries and biting winds, bringing the temperature down to around the minus nine degree mark.

We cleaned the weathering of snow and took the ice out of the baths and refilled them. The hawks were put out to weather, with care being taken to ensure they were on the side of the cottage that offered most protection from the wind. After a couple of hours' weathering, hawks and dogs were loaded up and we were off to the hill to try our luck at blue hares. The Harris and the female red tail were both capable of taking a blue hare, which is considerably smaller than a brown, but it might be asking a bit much of the male red tail. But he was normally a brave and determined hawk and it was felt that he ought to be given a crack at them.

We took the pointers with us as well as the springer spaniel, because of the large area we were going to need to cover to get sufficient flights. The plan was to walk line abreast with one pointer working each flank and the springer working the middle ground. The female hawks were put one at each end of the line with the male red tail in the middle.

Within a very short while we had two flights, in quick succession, at blue hares, both of which had turned white. Both hares managed to dump the hawks with consummate ease by employing the usual tactic of initially running downhill until the hawk made its first attack. Then the hares would stop dead, let the hawk overshoot, and turn and run for all they were worth uphill. The gap between hawk and hare increased rapidly and it was soon all over as far as the hawks were concerned. The pointers had locked on several times to grouse and we thought we might do better moving lower down the hill.

We dropped down slightly and carried on walking our line arrangement. We had another flight at a hare, which suffered the indignity of having fur removed from its rear end by the female red tail, although it still managed to evade the hawk and make good its escape. Next we crossed a track and put up a rabbit, which the male red tail took very well indeed. He followed every twist and turn of the rabbit and managed to latch hold with a yard or two to spare before it made safety.

We could feel that the weather was in for a change. The flurries had been coming and going and some were stronger than others. The sky immediately behind us was very dark, though we could see sunshine again behind it. It was clear that we were in for ten minutes or so of bad weather and then it would clear again. A little way off was a dip in the ground in which was a stand of half a dozen trees, so we made our way towards them in order to shelter the hawks from the impending snow. We had obviously chosen the right place as three roe deer burst from the sheltered spot as we entered. The flurry lasted barely ten minutes and then we set off again, completely dry. And, more importantly, the hawks were dry.

We moved down a gully and had to cross a small burn that ran through the bottom of it. Needless to say, despite warnings, one of our party fell in and got thoroughly soaked up to the chest. Every effort was made not to get the hawk wet but to no avail: she was sodden and the burn was ice cold. There was nothing for it but for the hapless individual to turn back and head for the vehicles. He needed to get home and get thoroughly dried off and into some fresh clothes, while the hawk would receive the attention of a hair drier and get fed up. It was far too cold to try to be macho and carry on hawking.

Personally, I felt that my wet friend should not be left to go back on his own, as we were by now over three miles from the vehicle. For those that are not used to the moors it is all too easy to become disorientated, so I accompanied him on his return route march. Also I must confess to being extremely worried about the hawk and felt it needed to be dried out and fed up as soon as possible. Once back at the cottage a bowl of warming soup and clean dry clothes for the falconer and a session with the hair drier and some food for the hawk saw everything put to rights.

I took advantage of this break in activities to fly the falcon on the creance. Now back to its normal self, it came promptly the full length of the creance. All being well, weather wise, I would fly it loose the next day.

The rest of the party returned some three-quarters of an hour later with the female Harris having taken a blue hare. Apparently she had learned her lesson from the brown one that had kicked her off and had taken this one with both feet around the head. The owner of the hawk was bubbling with happiness and that only left the female red without a kill that day.

There was sufficient daylight left to give her a decent go on some low ground we have permission on; because it is all close cover work, we left the pointers behind and just took the springer. Enthusiastic as ever, the springer worked the cover and soon flushed a rabbit for us. The female red tail was, on this occasion, a little slow off the mark and never really looked like catching this rabbit, but she made up for it on the next one and had it nailed within fifteen yards of being slipped. People often tell me that red tails are not very quick and are no good unless you fly them out of trees to give them the initial height advantage. But it would appear that no one has bothered to tell red tails that they are supposed to be slow. While they will undoubtedly benefit from being up a tree, as would any hawk, I cannot agree that they are slow. They might be slower than a goshawk and very slightly slower than a Harris' hawk, but they are certainly fast enough to give a monumental fear attack to most rabbits they chase.

Red tails also have another feature which helps them catch a lot of quarry that other hawks would miss: their willingness to commit themselves fully when chasing quarry and crash in where others may pull up short. It can lead to them injuring themselves on occasions, but I have yet to see a red tail that was indecisive when it came to the final moments of the chase. They give their all, and should be respected for it.

So apart from having one of our party taking an unscheduled bath it was, all in all, a very successful day. All the trained hawks had taken quarry and the falcon was ready to go loose. The goshawk was also starting to shape up and would be ready in a day or two.

The following day proved to be an interesting one for me, because the local keeper took me salmon fishing on the Spey. I have tried my hand at, and thoroughly enjoyed, trout fishing but never salmon. We stopped on the way so that I could hire a pair of waders and some lunch items for later. The Spey is a beautiful river and it felt really strange to wade out into it. It took me a time to get a hang of the casting method but eventually the fly was going roughly where I intended it to.

However, I did not manage to catch a fish or even get a close look at one. A salmon did leap out of the water just as we were deciding to call it a day, but I think this was a case of a fish taking the mickey. What did take the edge off my enjoyment was the waders that I had hired from a so-called reputable sports shop. One leg was fine, bone dry and surprisingly warm. The other leg leaked like a sieve and I was slopping around with a wet foot within seconds of first entering the water. When I took the waders back the person I returned them to said it was condensation, although how it could be condensation in only one leg is quite beyond me.

I got back in time to fly my falcon loose for the first time and I was extremely pleased with him. He is a gyr/peregrine hybrid and even during this short first flight showed the potential of his power. I flew him on the side of a hill up which the wind was blowing steadily. On leaving the fist he felt the wind under his sails and let himself be lifted up. I walked down the hill and he circled me, getting gradually higher all the while. When I considered that he had had enough for his first flight I waited till he was just past me going into the wind and yelled and threw the lure out on the ground. He folded his wings and came down like a rocket. In fact, he came in so fast that he overshot the lure and had to circle round again to get into it.

He hadn't been a tremendous height, probably no more than a hundred and fifty feet, but in the same circumstances he could easily have dropped down low to get under the wind. As he sat on the lure he was obviously not out of breath and was really good to take back up onto the fist. But then I always do put a lot of time into the initial training of my falcons. I can't stand a falcon with bad manners, particularly when it must nearly always be the trainer's own fault if they develop them.

On my return to the cottage the news that greeted me was that the red tails and harris hawk had had seven rabbits and the goshawk had been flown loose. With the goshawk it was a case of retraining as opposed to initial training, so the next day would see us endeavour to get her a decent slip at a rabbit.

Going out with the goshawk the next morning was a real pleasure. I had forgotten what fun gosses can be. This female was not a very big one: her flying weight was one pound fourteen ounces. Because we wanted to give her every chance of achieving an early kill and getting her confidence up we took a couple of ferrets out with us. I can't stand ferrets, and to be fair the majority I have met don't like me, but I was so keen to see the goshawk fly that I actually volunteered to do the ferreting.

We decided against taking any dogs with us as the hawk was slightly nervous of them. She would tolerate Rush, the springer spaniel, providing he didn't get too close to her but she would probably be put off by the pointers milling around. To be on the safe side all the dogs were left behind. The gos is only flown off the fist and not encouraged to take stand in a tree. I completely agreed with its owner on this point. It means that you, the falconer, are in control of the situation and any slip that might arise.

Having watched red tails and a harris hawk for the past few days it was all too easy to forget just how fast a goshawk can be when it means business. We ferreted a bury on the side of a hill and the rabbits flushed from it ran down the hill towards a wood some twenty yards away. The gos was off the fist at the first flicker of movement and had killed her first rabbit before it had got halfway to safety. Unlike some goshawks, this particular female is very well mannered on a kill and is nice and straightforward to pick up again – not something that can be said for all of them. Having been given a small reward we set off again to find another flight for her. The next bury we ferreted was considerably closer to the wood but we thought we would give it a try anyway.

This time the ferret reminded me of why I disliked ferreting so much. We could hear lots of thumping coming from under the ground but after fifteen minutes the ferret had failed to emerge. Needless to say it had killed and was probably feeding up a good way down under the frozen earth. I expressed my views on ferrets in general and this one in particular in no uncertain terms. The thought of trying to hack my way through the frozen ground to get to it was not filling me with loving thoughts towards it, but just as I started the task it came slowly wondering out of the hole, covered in fur and blood. For once in my life I was actually pleased to see one of these little creatures. At least I would not have to break my back digging for it.

We decided to move on to another piece of ground and see if we could find some rabbits out feeding although, with the weather being as cold as it was, it seemed an unlikely prospect. We thought it best not to put the ferret down a hole again that day so, having no dogs with us, I now took on the role of game finder. While my friend stood in what he thought was the best position, he would look on as I crashed around patches of rough ground and reed beds trying to push out a rabbit. I did manage to find several and we had some cracking flights. The goshawk displayed definite suicidal tendencies when it came to wire fences and other obstructions, though. Its policy seemed to be that if it flew into them hard enough it was bound to be able to come out the other side. Fortunately she did not injure herself and did manage to catch another rabbit.

The rapidity with which she would leave the fist and get up to her full speed was awesome. I thoroughly enjoyed myself and my companion was pleased that the gos was again going well. He called it a day at two kills as he wanted to feed her up and reward her well for her endeavours. We got back to the cottage just after lunch and were greeted with the news that the harris hawk had managed two rabbits and the male red tail one.

I still had plenty of daylight left in which to fly the falcon. I decided to take it up onto a nearby hill and fly it off the top. Having checked his telemetry was in good working order I cast him off into a good breeze. He started to go up and I walked slowly down the hill into a breeze that was blowing up it. This way it was making it very easy for him to gain height and he would be using more muscle to fly over the top of me. Everything was progressing as it should until a crow passed below some hundred yards or so in front of us. The falcon folded his wings and started to stoop. The crow had spotted the manoeuvre and easily evaded the onslaught to reach cover. Once safely ensconced in a tree it cawed at the circling falcon as if to tease it. I ran down and with some frantic stone-throwing managed to dislodge it. The chase was on again and this time the crow only just managed to make the safety of some cover. Having done so there was a marked absence of cawing. Perhaps he felt this time was just a little too close for comfort.

I called the falcon down to the lure and was surprised to see that he was not as out of breath as I thought he would be. Obviously he was puffing a bit, but not as much as I would have expected. The gyr/peregrine had taken on the flight at the crow without a moment's hesitation, so tomorrow we would go looking for some in circumstances that would be favourable for him.

The following day saw me out with my friend and his gos again in the morning. This time, thank god, no ferrets. As the gos had seemed to settle down considerably her owner decided to risk running the springer with her. As it turned out this did not present any problems, unless the springer got too close when the gos was on a kill. This was great as far as I was concerned because it meant I didn't have to do my impersonation of a dog or bring the ferret. I could just go along and enjoy myself.

We had a perfect start to the day's activities. As the gos was having its mews jesses changed for flying jesses we both spied a rabbit sneaking into a patch of cover. As quickly as we could we fitted the telemetry transmitter to the hawk's tail and set off to investigate. My friend manoeuvred himself into a good position and then the springer was encouraged to work the patch of ground. Sure enough, out popped the rabbit and the gos was on it in an instant: three minutes out in the field and we had had a kill. The gos was given a small reward before being taken back up on the fist. The springer tried to join in and have a share of the rabbit as well, but got a swipe across its nose from the goshawk for its trouble. It wouldn't be doing that again in a hurry.

We set off again in search of another flight and put up, or rather the springer put up, several brown hares. Each time one broke in front of us the goshawk was off the fist like a bullet, but on closing with the hare it would change its mind, swing round and come back to the fist. Very sensible, as this goshawk is not a very large one and a brown hare is a very powerful animal. Blue hares are a totally different prospect and most larger hawks should be able to hold them with relative ease – once, that is, they have learnt to grab them correctly. But a brown one can given even a large hawk a severe kicking.

We did not manage to find any more rabbits sitting out so we made our way to a reed bed that normally holds a rabbit or two, no matter what the time or weather conditions. This day was no exception and the springer soon flushed one for us. The gos chased this one hard but was just beaten. She came back to the fist and within minutes another was flushed for her. She saw it before we did and was off in a flash. It was a really good flight and, as the rabbit tried to make the cover of some small trees, the goshawk swerved between them and took the rabbit in fine style.

Again she was fed up on this kill as it is important to encourage a hawk and not overwork it. Also the flights had been good ones and deserved a reward. After all, falconry is supposed to be about the quality of the flight, not the total number of kills made, although it must be said that a confident hawk kills more than an unconfident one and confidence normally comes from fitness and success. The falconer with the goshawk was returning home the next day so the gos was given a full gorge on this last rabbit. While it was taking its pleasure the jesses were changed back and the leash and swivel put on. This time the dog was allowed a portion of warm rabbit as well. After all, he had played his part in the success of the day.

In the afternoon it was out with Luther the gyr/peregrine hybrid. Our starting point was on the top of a high hill that overlooked a pleasant valley where rooks and crows could often be seen feeding in the bottom. As this was our first real attempt to catch one we were looking for circumstances that would favour the falcon and put the corvid at a disadvantage.

Before taking the falcon out of the car we scanned the ground below us with binoculars. There were several parties of rooks and one or two crows, but all were too close to cover to give the falcon a reasonable chance. In the excitement of the occasion it is all too easy to accept a situation that is second best and normally the falconer ends up regretting his actions. I was determined to wait for the right slip and settled down to watch and wait. The falcon was in its transport box in the back of the car, so there were no flapping wings to give our intentions away. Jesses had already been changed over and the telemetry transmitter fitted to its tail.

We watched and waited for more than an hour. Our patience was eventually rewarded when a small group of four rooks gradually got closer to us and further away from cover. When I considered that they were at least twice as far from cover as they were from us I carefully made my way back to the car and got the falcon. The plan was to put him in the air just over the skyline from the rooks. I would then run forward and by the time he swung up over me he would be above them and they would have to fly directly into the wind to reach cover. The advantage should then be with the falcon.

Strange how these things, no matter how deliberately you set about them, never ever go to plan. Luther was put on the wing and I ran forward to crest the hill. My presence alerted the rooks and away they flew. According to plan they battled into the wind to reach a small copse some considerable distance away. I looked above so that I could enjoy the sight of a large falcon arrowing its way across the sky in deadly pursuit of its quarry. No falcon.

By the time I realised there was no falcon above me I had run a considerable distance down the hill. I waited a while for Luther to appear but it was a vain wait. I went back up to the top of the hill, but at nowhere near the same speed that I had started to come down it. I assumed that the falcon had not crested the rise and as a result had got blown downwind. I swung the lure and called but the falcon did not appear, so it was out with the telemetry receiver. Thankfully there was a strong signal. The falcon was downwind but not too far away, and it was also possible to tell from the signal that he was stationary.

Accordingly I set off to recover my falcon, walking towards the signal, and my companions took the vehicle and headed in the general direction I was walking. It turned out that the falcon was further away than I had expected. From the strength of the signal I was getting I thought he was about half to three-quarters of a mile away but, as it transpired, I was getting a more or less line of sight signal. He was actually nearer three miles away. As I got closer to him, which was evident from the signal the telemetry receiver was giving, I couldn't understand why he didn't come in to the lure. I started to have the terrible thoughts that all falconers have from time to time. I imagined everything that could have happened to him. He had flown into a sheep fence and broken his neck. He had landed on the ground and been grabbed by a fox. A golden eagle had killed him. All sorts of dreadful thoughts were running through my mind.

When I did eventually get to him he was standing up, large as life, with a bulging crop. Beside him was the well-eaten carcase of a crow. Not being one of life's optimists, I assumed he had spotted a dead one on the ground and had come down for an easy meal. In fact I cursed him under my breath as I made in to him to pick him up. (I say made into him gently because he had a full crop and if he were to take flight the consequences would not be good.) It was then that I noticed his chest was speckled with blood and his feet were covered in it. I put a hand on the crow and it was still warm. He had obviously spotted it when I cast him off and had gone directly for it. My curses now changed to praises and I was extremely pleased with Luther. My only regret was that I had not seen the flight.

Once safely back on the fist I gave Luther a thorough check over. A crow is a powerful adversary and until a falcon learns how to grab them correctly they can all too easily inflict injuries. But Luther appeared well and injury free. Many years ago I had a saker/peregrine hybrid falcon that got badly beaten up by a crow. It took several months for her to recover fully from her injuries, and I assumed that she would be useless as a hunting falcon after this episode. But, as it turned out, quite the reverse was true, for she would fly any corvid with gusto thereafter.

Luther had too large a crop to fly the next day so it would be the day after that we would try again. The following day he was fed a smaller ration than usual, as soon as he had cast the remains of the previous day's meal. In this way I hoped he would be ready early on the following day. As it turned out, a day's rest would be no bad thing.

The friends who had been staying and hunting with me were making preparations to set off for the long journey back home, so there was plenty to do. Other friends with red tails would be arriving that evening and there were obviously things to do to be ready for them. Only the falconer with the female harris hawk was staying on. He had been due to go back with the others, but his hawk was going so well and he was enjoying himself so much that he decided to risk the wrath of his wife and stay on a bit longer.

The friends with the red tails duly arrived and settled themselves, hawks, dogs and ferrets in their temporary home. As well as a male and female red tail hawk they had also brought along a male harris hawk. All three hawks were young hawks of the season. The harris hawk was a screamer and was consequently weathered away from the other hawks. I have to admit that a screaming hawk or falcon is not something that I could live with personally, but it doesn't seem to bother some people.

My friends had also brought three dogs with them, two springers and a German short haired pointer. With my two pointers as well the kennels were straining at the seams, but fortunately the mews we have will take any number of hawks so the extra harris did not present a real problem (other than to our nerves).

The hawks all set off in a large party the following morning and I set off on my own with the falcon. When I got to the ground where I intended to hunt I had to re-evaluate my day's plans, because a large wild peregrine falcon was hunting in earnest where I had intended to fly. No doubt things would settle down fairly quickly but even so everything in the area would be nervous for a while. The keeper of this particular estate is always exceedingly helpful and I drove over to see him and explained the situation. I could have gone to another part of the estate that would have been suitable, but it was too close to where the hawks were being flown. The last thing we wanted was to have an accident of that nature.

The keeper phoned another keeper on a nearby estate and it was very soon agreed I could go across and fly my falcon at corvids there. The keeper was very keen to see a trained falcon in action and I asked if he would mind if we used his vehicle to go out over the estate. After all, the local rooks and crows would be used to seeing his vehicle and we would probably get closer than with my car.

He readily agreed and after a cup of tea we set off. I explained to him what we needed in terms of wind direction and positioning of rooks in relation to cover. I had decided to slip Luther out of the vehicle window. In this way I hoped we would obtain an easy slip for him. After all, he had only one crow to his credit and I wasn't sure of the circumstances in which he had taken it. But he had shown twice now that he was keen to take corvids on and that was the main thing. If we could get him two or three more in quick succession he should end up completely wedded to them.

The keeper very soon got us into a position where a flight was possible. Luther was kitted out with telemetry, ready to go. I asked the keeper to go on driving slowly, as opposed to stopping, in the hope of taking the rooks completely unawares. This he did and at the critical moment I struck the braces on Luther's hood. I eased my arm out of the window and then removed the hood completely. Luther bobbed his head twice and was off. Some rooks, in the not too far distance, were moving position slightly. They would lift up and go down again within a few yards. This movement had attracted Luther's attention and he was making straight for the group. On his approach the rooks took flight and separated into two groups.

Luther closed rapidly on the group nearest to him and then, at the last moment, switched his attention to the other group. This was his undoing. For what reason he switched groups I will never know – perhaps he thought he had spotted one that was weak on the wing or ailing in some way. Anyway, he failed to catch one before they made cover and the other group were now too far away from him to get on terms with them. He did briefly give chase, but once he realised it was futile he turned and headed back to us. I threw out the lure and called him down. When he had taken a small reward from the lure I took him up on the fist and hooded him.

The keeper and I sat in the vehicle for a while having a smoke and a chat while we allowed Luther half an hour to get himself rested sufficiently for another flight. We set off again in search of some more rooks and it didn't take too long to come across another group. But this was a large scattered flock containing rooks and crows and I felt it would not make a good slip for Luther. It would be hard for him to focus instantly on a specific target once the hood was removed. I have found previously that large flocks very often tend to confuse a falcon. Even a few moment's hesitation can make the difference between success and failure, so it was decided to press on and look for another slip.

It didn't take long and soon we were approaching a small group out feeding well away from any cover. Also we were approaching them directly into the wind, so the flight should go according to plan. The same tactics as before were employed and Luther was slipped out of the vehicle window. He flew directly at them and for some reason one of the group was very late in rising. Luther bound to it after it had only travelled a few yards and kill number two was in the bag. But it had hardly been a taxing or a particularly sporting one. I decided not to feed him up as I would normally have done as no great effort had gone into the flight. I would allow him another brief rest period and then see if we could get another flight.

The one encouraging feature of the brief flight was the manner in which the quarry had been taken by Luther. He had grabbed the rook and pulled it to the ground where he had immediately transferred his grip to its head. This way he could despatch the quarry quickly and not risk injury to himself. One of the features of hybrids is their willingness to tackle quarry such as rooks and crows on the ground. A lot of straight peregrine falcons will beat rooks in the air but shy away from them once they have been put down on the ground. At the very least they usually hit them once or twice more before coming in on them. All of the larger hybrids, on the other hand, seem perfectly happy to get straight in and mix it.

We did manage to get one more flight that day and it was a much better one. I used the same method of obtaining a flight as before but this time Luther had to work hard to get on terms with his rook. He put in a short stoop and made an effort to grab the rook. It managed to evade this action, turned and took off for all it was worth downwind, but Luther managed to overhaul it before it reached sanctuary and took it well. This time he did get a full crop on his kill. The keeper was happy as he had two less rooks on his ground and I was happy that Luther hadn't hesitated to fly corvids at any given opportunity.

Meanwhile the harris hawks and the red tails had been having some excellent sport and the local rabbit population had suffered a few setbacks. No doubt they would recover quickly enough. Several blue hares had been taken and the female red tail had managed to catch and hold a brown hare. Everybody was happy and had thoroughly enjoyed their stay in Scotland.

Luther progressed well with his short campaign against corvids and caught several more. But, more important than just catching them, he was catching them with style. The flights were excellent to watch and his flying skills got better literally day by day. His last kill, before I came back down south, was one that only a hybrid falcon would have made. He had flown a crow and it had been a good flight with much aerial manoeuvring. The crow had just managed to make the cover of a fir tree and once in its branches started to call its annoyance at the falcon. Unlike a peregrine, which would have called this flight a day, Luther gained some height and then stooped straight in among the branches and grabbed a crow. It was a fitting end to our stay in Scotland.

# CHAPTER TEN

# Tail piece

MY life in falconry has been a very full and satisfying one – not that I hope it is going to be over just yet! I have spent a great deal of my adult life travelling the globe to experience first hand different branches of falconry. I have probably visited more than twenty countries either to watch or participate in various forms of falconry. A comment that I receive a great deal is that I am fortunate to lead the life that I do. This annoys me intensely. When I was a great deal younger I took a conscious decision about what I wanted to do with my life and altered things accordingly. I gave up a very well-paid career, taking a 75 per cent drop in living standards initially, but the quality of my life increased by a great deal more than the corresponding loss of finance.

Luck does play a major part in our lives, but it is possible to make some of your own. Falconry means more to me than fast cars, expensive clothes and other such trappings of a so-called successful life. Now I spend every day of my life doing what I want to do, which is to fly hawks and falcons here in the UK and to travel abroad and see others doing the same when our game season is closed.

I think that falconry does get under the skin and tends to push everything else into the background. The true falconer probably verges on the fanatical. He or she is always striving to improve their technique with their hawks and to increase their understanding of them. People often talk about the good old days of falconry, as if they are long past. I think that there are currently a number of falconers who are as good as any there have ever been, but with the growing popularity of the sport and the ease with which hawks can now be obtained there are also more dabblers than there have ever been before. Falconers do not class these people as fellow sportsmen. But to the general public, anybody with a hawk is automatically a falconer. I find it frightening to have conversations with people who have had five or six hawks in barely as many months. Some would appear to change hawks as often as some of us change clothes.

Most things in life have a negative and a positive side and the domestic production of raptors and telemetry are two good examples. Domestic production means that the wild stock of raptors can be left in peace and falconers can fulfil their own needs entirely. But it also means that there is often a surplus of hawks and falcons that find their way into entirely unsuitable hands. When it was a little more difficult to obtain hawks the process automatically weeded out a great many people who were just not suited to owning them. Now if somebody has a whim and desires a hawk they will probably be able to get one – not a good situation for the hawk involved.

Telemetry has doubtless led to the recovery of many a lost hawk. But what has happened to the field craft that pre–telemetry falconers employed when they lost a hawk? It has all but gone. I know of someone who recently lost a falcon and the transmitter stopped working after it had been out for about forty minutes. This person literally gave up the search. He told me that without a transmitter there was absolutely no chance of recovering the falcon and therefore there was no point in looking. Another local falconer and I went out with him and we managed to locate the falcon and get it back for him. The person who had lost the falcon was stunned: you would have thought that we had been practising black magic. He had no idea of how to go about looking for a falcon and what signs in nature to take notice of. He had grown up in a world of telemetry transmitters and was totally lost without them.

My own hopes for the future are to move to Scotland and fly peregrine falcons that I have bred and hacked myself. I have found a lovely cottage in an isolated situation and secured the rights to fly on some beautiful low ground and moorland. My friend Roger Ratcliffe's peregrines bred with mine this year, so I am two-thirds of the way there. It has taken many years to find the right cottage in the right location and an equal number of years to breed the peregrines. But no doubt someone will tell me I am lucky to do what I do.

Falconry has given me a very great deal in life. It has introduced me to some wonderful people and given me literally thousands of hours of pleasure. Long may it continue to do so.

# GLOSSARY

**Accipiter**   Hawk typically having short rounded wings and a long tail.

**Anatum peregrine**   American subspecies of peregrine.

**Backing (dogs)**   The term used when one pointer comes on point behind another and is said to 'back the point'.

**Bald eagle**   North American fish-eating eagle.

**Barbary falcon**   A small, Middle Eastern subspecies of peregrine.

**Bate**   When a hawk or falcon hurls itself from the fist or perch in an attempt to fly off.

**Booted eagle**   Small European eagle feeding mainly on snakes.

**Brookie**   Small Mediterranean subspecies of peregrine falcon.

**Blocks**   Vertical cylindrical perches used by trained falcons out of doors.

**Bow perch**   Perch in the shape of a bow, as near a natural branch shape as possible, used for trained hawks out of doors.

**Braces**   Thin leather straps used to open and close a falcon's hood.

**Cadge**   A light wooden frame which enables a falconer to carry several hooded falcons in the field at one time.

**Cast off**   The moment of release when a hawk or falcon leaves the falconer's fist.

**Calidus peregrine**   Siberian subspecies of peregrine.

**Clip to the glove**   To attach the hawk or falcon to the glove in preparation for flight, after it has had its normal furniture removed.

**Cooper's hawk**   North American accipiter similar to the European sparrowhawk.

**Corvid**   A member of the crow family.

**Covey**   A family party of game birds, such as grouse or partridge.

**Creance**   Training line used for calling the hawk or falcon prior to its being flown completely free.

**Crop**   The sac, at the top of the gullet, where food is first stored when eaten by falcons and hawks.

**Drop in condition**   To lower a hawk's general condition and put an edge on its appetite.

**Enter at quarry**   The first time a hawk flies at a particular quarry and kills it.

**Eyass**   Young hawk or falcon in its first year.

**Falcon**   A long-winged, dark-eyed bird of prey, with a characteristic notch in the upper beak.

**Ferruginous hawk**   Large North American hawk believed by some ornithologists to be closer to an eagle than a hawk.

**Flush**   To make the game run or fly for the hawk or falcon to chase.

**Fly at check**   When a hawk or falcon switches from the quarry that has been selected for it to another it has chosen for itself.

**Foot the falconer**   When a hawk or falcon grabs the falconer's free hand; normally as a result of carelessness on the part of the falconer.

**Get a foot to**   When a hawk or falcon clutches its prey.

**Golden eagle**   One of the largest and most powerful eagles, with wide distribution throughout the northern hemisphere.

**Goshawk**   Large accipiter found throughout the northern hemisphere. Very popular as a falconry bird.

**Grey phase gyr**   The northern European colour phase of the gyr falcon.

**Gyr falcon**   The largest and most powerful member of all the falcon family.

**Gyrlin**   Hybrid falcon produced by crossing a gyr falcon with a merlin.

**Hack board**   An artificial feeding sight for falcons that have been put out to hack.

**Haggard**   A hawk or falcon taken from the wild in adult plumage for the purpose of falconry. This is now illegal in Great Britain.

**Harris' hawk**   American raptor that has found a unique niche in falconry. Probably the most widely used hawk in Great Britain at the present time.

**Head the point**   To get in front and upwind of the dog, when it is pointing game, in preparation for the flush.

**Hecking**   The sound made by falcons to show their displeasure.

**Hybrid falcon**   A bird produced, normally by artificial insemination, by crossing two species, such as gyr/peregrine, saker/peregrine, etc.

**Imp up**   The process of repairing broken flight feathers in a falconer's bird.

**Imprint**   To replace the parent bird with a human in the mind of a young bird.

**Jerkin**   Male of the gyr falcon.

**Jesses**   Leather straps by which the hawk is fettered.

**Killed over**   A dog is regarded as having been 'killed over' when it has produced game for a hawk or falcon, and the quarry has been killed as a result of the dog's efforts.

**Lanner falcon**   An African and European falcon that is somewhat smaller than a peregrine.

**Lanneret**   Male lanner falcon.

**Lappet faced vulture**   One of the largest members of the vulture family.

**Line abreast**   When several people walk in a line, side by side, to flush game.

**Line of sight signal**   The range of a telemetry set when there is nothing to disturb the signal.

**Lugger falcon**   A medium-sized falcon from the subcontinent of India.

**Lure**   The artificial bird, normally made of leather, which is used to recall the falcon after an unsuccessful flight.

**Macropus peregrine**   Australian subspecies of peregrine.

**Make in to**   To gently approach a hawk or falcon when it is on a kill or the lure.

**Make to the hood**   The process of initially making a hawk or falcon accept the wearing of a hood.

**Malprinted**   When the imprinting process has gone wrong and the young hawk or falcon has become fixated on food.

**Manning**   The process of calming a new hawk or falcon, and literally getting it used to man and everything that goes with human society.

**Merlin**   Small falcon found throughout the northern hemisphere. Traditionally used in falconry for the flight at skylarks.

**Musket**   Male sparrowhawk.

**Mute**   The droppings of a hawk.

**On quarry**   When a hawk or falcon sits on its prey at the end of a successful flight.

**On the soar**   When a bird of prey circles higher and higher on a thermal, out of control of the falconer.

**Passage hawk**   Bird still in immature plumage when trapped on its first migration, for the purpose of falconry. This is now illegal in Great Britain.

**Peales peregrine**   Canadian subspecies of peregrine.

**Peregrine falcon**   Large falcon with worldwide distribution. Since time immemorial the prized bird of falconers.

**Perlin**   Hybrid falcon produced by crossing a peregrine falcon and a merlin.

**Pick up piece**   A piece of meat used by the falconer to literally pick the falcon or hawk up off its kill or the lure.

**Point**   The action of a dog freezing having found game.

**Prairie falcon**   North American falcon in the same size range as the peregrine.

**Put on the wing**   When a falcon is allowed to take flight from the glove, normally in game hawking.

**Put out to hack**   When young falcons are put out for several weeks' liberty prior to being taken up and trained.

**Quarter the ground**   The side to side running pattern used by a pointer in its search for game.

**Raptor**   Bird of prey.

**Red headed merlin**   Small falcon found in India and Africa. Not really a member of the merlin family at all.

**Red naped shaheen**   Middle Eastern falcon, slightly smaller than the peregrine, to which it is closely related.

**Ring up**   The circling action used by a falcon to get high up above dog or falconer in expectation of being served with prey.

**Rouse**   The action of a hawk or falcon shaking all its feathers and settling them back into place before flying.

**Saker**   Large falcon found in the Middle East and the Steppes.

**Slip**   Each attempt at wild quarry with a trained hawk or falcon.

**Slipping order**   Used when several falconers are hunting together, so that two hawks are not inadvertently put in the air together.

**Social imprint**   To take the imprinting process a stage further so that the hawk in question can be used for artificial insemination work.

**Staunch point**   When a pointer locks on solidly to game.

**Stoop**   The dramatic dive of the falcon after its prey.

**Swivel**   A small metal device used between the jesses and leash to stop a hawk or falcon getting tangled whilst on its perch.

**Take stand**   Said of a hawk when it has missed its quarry and goes off and perches in a tree. It is often reluctant to come down again promptly.

**Telemetry**   Radio tracking system used by falconers to recover lost hawks.

**Tiercel**   Term now used generally to refer to the male of hawks and falcons, but more correctly only applies to the male peregrine.

**Tyro**   Beginner or novice.

**Vulture**   Large carrion-eating bird of prey.

**Waiting on**   The action of a falcon circling the falconer in expectation of being served with game.

**Weather**   To sit hawks outside to allow them to 'take the weather'.

**Weatherings**   The outside accommodation for trained hawks and falcons.